AN ARTS FOUNDATION COURSE

UNITS 13–15
INTRODUCTION TO PHILOSOPHY

*Prepared by Stuart Brown and Janet Radcliffe Richards
for the Course Team*

The Open
University

Cover illustration: John Stuart Mill (1806–1873), from *Illustrated London News*, March, 1866

Contributors

Stuart Brown has written the Preface and Part I; Janet Radcliffe Richards has written Part II.

The Open University
Walton Hall, Milton Keynes
MK7 6AA

First edition published 1986, second edition published 1988, third edition published 1990. Reprinted 1992, 1994, 1995

Designed by the Graphic Design Group of the Open University

Printed in Great Britain by Page Bros, Norwich

ISBN 0 7492 1044 3

This text forms part of an Open University course. The complete list of units in the course appears on the back cover of this text.

For general availability of supporting material referred to in this text, please write to Open University Educational Enterprises Limited, 12 Cofferidge Close, Stony Stratford, Milton Keynes, MK11 1BY, United Kingdom.

Further information on Open University courses may be obtained from The Open University, PO Box 625, Walton Hall, Milton Keynes, MK1 1TY

3.4

Units 13–15

INTRODUCTION TO PHILOSOPHY

SET READING

As you work through these units you will need to refer to
John Golby (ed.) (1986) *Culture and Society in Britain 1850–1890* (Course Reader)
Charles Dickens (1989 edn) *Hard Times* (Set Book)
Broadcast Notes
Cassette Notes

BROADCASTING

Television programme 13 *Utilitarianism: a lecture by Bernard Williams*
Television programme 14 *Utilitarianism: a tutorial with Rohan Collier*
Television programme 15 *Victorian Ways of Death*
Radio programme 7 *Free Will discussed*

CASSETTE

Cassette 2 side 2 band 3 *What Philosophy is: an Introduction*

PREFACE

Works of philosophy are in some respects superficially similar to works of art. There are great philosophical works of the past (like the dialogues of Plato) that occupy the same kind of special position in European culture as do great works of art, music and literature. Indeed, even if the word 'literature' were reserved for writing of a certain quality, some works of philosophy would also be works of literature. Novels, like works of philosophy, consist of sequences of sentences that, generally speaking, are meant to be understood. The methods of analysis and criticism employed in philosophy can be used in literature and vice versa. From a negative point of view, the thought in a novel can be confused and the writing of a philosopher can be unimaginative. And novelists will not usually be talented philosophers or vice versa. Charles Dickens, as we will see, has no aptitude or taste for philosophy. But it is not difficult to find examples of people who excel in both literature and philosophy – Jean-Paul Sartre and Iris Murdoch, to give two contemporary examples. This is, I am suggesting, to be expected given the obvious fact that philosophers are writers.

In spite of such overlaps and similarities, however, philosophy is practised differently from the study of literature. When you study a poem you may be encouraged to look for its strengths and weaknesses. But if you are led to see, for instance, that it has a weak ending, you are not then invited to construct an alternative ending. If you study a passage of philosophy you are also likely to be encouraged to look for strengths and weaknesses in its argument. But being critical in philosophy involves asking yourself what you would have said, whether you could produce a better argument. You will find an increasing emphasis on this kind of participation as you work through the material in these units. Of course, you will be learning about philosophy as well. But increasingly, and especially in Part II, you will be learning to philosophize. Here you will be engaged in the much-debated problem of free will and determinism.

This emphasis on active participation is present also in Part I of these units. Here you will be considering the ideas of two important British philosophers of the nineteenth century. One aim of this part is to give you some sense of the cultural significance of philosophy by looking at these writings in a wider context. Another is to set the scene for your study of the social and political thought of John Stuart Mill in an interdisicplinary context later in the course. But the aspect of the thought of these philosophers we shall be studying – known as 'utilitarianism' – remains an important though controversial part of moral and social thinking in our time. For this reason you should find the transition from thinking critically about Mill to thinking where you stand in the controversy a fairly smooth one.

At the same time philosophy has changed a good deal over the past century, just as have all other disciplines. I shall say more later (Section 5) about what has changed since Mill's time. Here I would like in a preliminary way only to stress one central feature of serious philosophy from Plato to the present day and to note one respect in which philosophy has changed since the last century.

We have already noted that philosophy, like literature, uses the medium of the written (or spoken) word. And I am sure that, even if you have not studied any philosophy before, you already know that philosophers mostly use the medium in a different way and for different ends. If you wanted to find a work of philosophy in your local library you would, I am sure, not look under 'Fiction'. Those who write philosophy are not trying to entertain, as writers of fiction often are, but to instruct, convince or in some other way persuade their readers. Perhaps there are philosophy groups that are nothing more than coteries of like-minded people who help to reinforce curious opinions in each other. But the mark of serious philosophers is their willingness to challenge assertions for which no argument has been given and, on the other side, to take up the challenge. It is very appropriate that the literary form many serious philosophers, including Plato, have chosen is the dialogue.

Argument is of course a central part of any academic discipline and any essay you write is supposed to take the form of a sustained argument. In other subjects, like history, the argument may consist in drawing the conclusions you are entitled to draw on the basis of the available evidence. In learning how to evaluate different kinds of source in history you have been learning something of the methods historians use. Other disciplines have different methods. What is special about argument in philosophy is that it is often difficult to produce arguments about the matters discussed and sometimes it is even unclear whether the matters admit of rational discussion at all.

Philosophers have discussed, for instance, the question as to what the rational basis is for distinguishing morally right actions from those that are morally wrong. That question is about how you can argue that a particular action is morally right. Philosophers as we shall see in Part I of these units, have proposed different criteria for judging actions to be right and wrong. And, more recently, there have been those who have held that judgements of right and wrong are wholly subjective – that therefore there is no rational basis for morality. Philosophical ethics is, according to this view, a waste of time. But someone who says it is a waste of time because there is no rational basis for it is actually adopting a philosophical position. If we ask his reasons and he has none then we have no reason to believe him. Once, however, he starts giving reasons for believing that there is no rational basis for morality he is actually doing philosophy, even contributing, ironically, to philosophical ethics.

The example I have given, as well as illustrating how argument features centrally in serious philosophy, may also serve to bring out one respect in which philosophy now is different from philosophy in the Victorian Britain of John Stuart Mill. For Mill was quite confident that it was possible to provide – indeed that he had succeeded in providing – a rational basis for morality. Mill's confidence is not one we can share. The role of the philosopher, the tone he or she can adopt in talking or writing to others has changed.

That is not to say that philosophers nowadays think that morality is all subjective or that it is impossible to reason at all about moral matters. But scepticism about whether it is possible to reason about moral matters has been part of the changed context for twentieth-century philosophy and represents one respect in which our culture is different from that of the Victorians. I say 'our culture' deliberately. For part of what philosophers do at any given time is to articulate assumptions and predelictions that are very widely shared in the community in order to consider whether it is reasonable to hold them. I have mentioned the temptation to believe that questions of morality do not admit of rational discussion because I hoped that example would ring a bell with you, even if you think the temptation should be resisted. In that same way we hope that in each of the two parts of this 'Introduction to Philosophy' we will be dealing with topics about which you may find you have opinions already. It is not so easy to look for reasons for what you are already inclined to believe or for not accepting what someone else is inclined to believe. But even this need not be too difficult where, as you should find in Part I, the paths are already well-trodden.

PART I   UTILITARIANISM

INTRODUCTION

Those who first coined the word 'utilitarian' assumed that religion was the only proper basis for morality and the word 'utilitarian' was initially applied to someone who rejected religion. Such a person, it was assumed, was therefore devoid of morality and was rather given to the ruthless pursuit of wealth and other material gains. When John Stuart Mill adopted the term 'utilitarianism' it seems he was at least partly willing to accept that it was a rival to Church Christianity. As we shall see, he did not accept the assumption that the only proper foundation for morality is religion. He tried to show, on the contrary, that there could be a 'secular' (i.e. non-religious) morality, that indeed human happiness was the true criterion of right and wrong. The spread of utilitarianism may be seen as one aspect of a cultural phenomenon sometimes referred to as 'secularization', in which specifically religious ideas, institutions and symbols are replaced by ones that are not specifically religious. Television programme 15 'Victorian Ways of Death' provides some striking examples of such 'secularization' of Christian symbols. In the case of utilitarianism it is the concept of human happiness that is secularized. Whereas human happiness in religious terms was thought to be found in communion with God and perhaps only fully to be attained in an afterlife, the utilitarians took happiness in a worldly sense, often identifying it with pleasure.

The utilitarians made a particular impact in the early nineteenth century, virtually forming themselves into a distinct political party. It seems likely that Dickens's character Thomas Gradgrind was intended as a caricature of a utilitarian MP. To that extent *Hard Times* may be seen as a satire of early utilitarianism. Dickens and J. S. Mill were, however, almost contemporaries and were to some extent exposed to the same influences. *Hard Times,* for example, is inscribed to Thomas Carlyle, himself a severe critic of utilitarianism. In spite of Carlyle's hostility to the way of thinking that Mill was brought up in, both managed to be on quite friendly terms. And, while he never took to Carlyle's style of writing and denied that he learnt much directly from Carlyle, Mill admitted that he came round in other ways to recognizing truth in what Carlyle had to say. Thus Mill's utilitarianism is rather different from that of the early utilitarians since it is modified to take account of those criticisms Mill thought needed to be taken seriously.

In this part we will begin by considering early utilitarianism as formulated by Jeremy Bentham (1748–1832). We will look at some of the criticisms made of early utilitarianism by such as Carlyle and Dickens in order to see why they were made and how far they reach their target. We will then look at what is regarded as the 'classic' statement of utilitarianism – that of J. S. Mill in his essay *Utilitarianism* (1863). We will consider whether Mill succeeds in showing that utilitarianism can meet the difficulties raised by its critics.

Utilitarianism is not, however, just a way of thinking that became prominent in the nineteenth century. In a modified form it not only survives in our own time but has probably become the most influential moral and social philosophy. So much so that you might well be a utilitarian already, even if you have not heard the name before. On the other hand you may, as some do, find yourself repelled by it. I hope that, if you think utilitarianism is just obviously right, you will, by the end of these units, come to see that there are difficulties for this way of thinking that need to be overcome. If, on the other hand, your immediate reaction is that there is 'something wrong' with it, I hope that you will be able to convert your hunch that something is wrong into arguments against utilitarianism. Since hunches are not always right you may, of course, find that the utilitarian is able to reply to your arguments. That process of argument and counter-argument is characteristic of doing philosophy.

1 JEREMY BENTHAM AND EARLY UTILITARIANISM

Utilitarianism can be stated very loosely as that way of thinking according to which the *only* test of whether something is right or wrong is whether or not it produces happiness or reduces pain. The slogan 'the greatest happiness of the greatest number' dates back to the eighteenth century and there are several distinguished British philosophers of that period whose moral and social thought can be classed as broadly 'utilitarian'. But the utilitarianism of Jeremy Bentham took a distinctive form that owed much to French influences, in particular to the writings of Claude-Adrien Helvétius (1715–71). It was both anti-religious and politically radical. It was anti-religious to the extent that it sought an alternative basis for moral thinking from that offered by the Church. It was politically radical to the extent that it defined the 'public interest' in terms of 'the greatest happiness of the greatest number' and called in question the pretension of those who governed to be acting in the 'public interest'. Helvétius published his ideas in a book in 1758 but it was immediately seen as both heretical and subversive. Copies of it were publicly burned and further publication suppressed. This, of course, only served to make something of a martyr out of Helvétius and to increase the interest in his writings when they eventually became available.

Neither tyranny nor religious intolerance was practised in Bentham's Britain on the scale of pre-Revolution France. There was some discrimination. Bentham, to his life-long regret, made a false statement of adherence to the 39 Articles of the Church of England in order to gain admittance to the University of Oxford. Catholics were not admitted to political office until 1828. But Bentham's Britain was no tyranny. Nor was it a democracy. Only a small number of men of property had the right to elect Members of Parliament. There was a political and religious establishment which governed Britain and constituted what Bentham called 'the sinister interest'. Bentham and the 'Philosophical Radicals', as they were called, sought to reduce the power enjoyed by this small group of people.

1.1 THE 'GREATEST HAPPINESS' PRINCIPLE

The phrase 'the greatest happiness of the greatest number' is a vague one but we have already seen two ways in which it takes on a more precise meaning for Bentham and his followers. In the first place it means the happiness people seek in this life and not in an afterlife. There had been religious philosophers who represented God as concerned to produce the greatest happiness of the greatest number, taking human happiness to consist ultimately in the salvation of human souls. But that idea of happiness, in which it is truly to be found in an afterlife, plays no part in Bentham's thinking. Bentham was not indeed concerned to distinguish between the pursuit of happiness and, for instance, the pursuit of pleasure. This is clear in the definition he gives of 'utility':

> By utility is meant that property in any object, whereby it tends to produce benefit, ·
> advantage, pleasure, good, or happiness, *(all this in the present case comes to the same
> thing)* or *(what again comes to the same thing)* to prevent the happening of mischief,
> pain, evil, or unhappiness to the party whose interest is considered... (See below,
> Section 1.3)

Notice that Bentham is not saying that there is no difference between happiness, pleasure and so on. His point is only that nothing turns on the difference so far as concerns his utilitarianism. Nothing turns on it because Bentham is concerned with what they have in common, namely, that human beings are naturally attracted by what makes them happy, gives them pleasure, and so on. Equally, though there

Figure 1 Jeremy Bentham (1748–1823). the founder of english Utilitariahnism as a movement for social, legal and constitutional reform. His main works were Fragment on Government (1776) and Introduction to thie Principles of Morals and Legislation (1789). (Photo: Fotomax Index, London)

are differences between pain, evil, and so on that Bentham need not deny, he is interested in what they have in common, namely, that people are naturally repelled by them. So Bentham is far from those philosophers who have built their moral theories on a fundamental distinction between happiness (which is lasting) and pleasure (which is short-lived) as religious philosophers often have done.

A second respect in which 'utility' is given a sharper definition by Bentham than by some earlier utilitarians is that he would not allow vague appeals to 'the welfare of the people as a whole', 'the public interest', or whatever, as if society as a whole was greater than the sum of its parts. Such appeals by a nation's leaders could, in Bentham's eyes, easily result in their pretending to look after 'the welfare of the people as a whole' when in reality they were acting contrary to the interests of the great majority. For Bentham, a society simply consists of the individuals that are in it and there can be no more to the happiness of a society than the happiness of those individuals. If that is so, and if we pass over differences between what makes people more happy and what they prefer, then to govern in 'the public interest' is to govern in accordance with what most people prefer. Governments ought, in short, to be subject to something like democratic control. Otherwise government will only promote the interests of the governing classes. Utilitarianism, as put forward by Bentham, has the implication that everyone ought to have a share in the political process. Bentham accepted this implication. Doubtless there would be certain classes of people to be excluded – children, prisoners and the insane – each for particular reasons. But Bentham did not envisage that women would be excluded.

1.2 BENTHAM AND THE CRIMINAL LAW

Such constitutional reform was only one part of the programme of reform that Bentham envisaged. He was particularly concerned with the reform of the criminal law and it is in this area of reform that Bentham was most influential. For a utilitarian, no action is good or bad in itself but only in virtue of tending to produce a good or bad result. It is the *consequences* of an action – in particular its *effects* on happiness – that make it right or wrong. So, for instance, there is nothing inherently right about punishing someone who has committed a crime. On the contrary, punishment could *only* be justified if the harm done by punishing the offender was outweighed by some benefit. For instance, if other people were sufficiently deterred from committing a similar crime by the knowledge that anyone found guilty would be punished – that is the sort of justification a utilitarian, Bentham included, could accept. Punishment had to be justified by its consequences. It was not justified merely by the fact that someone had been found guilty of a crime. It was not justified merely as an act of retribution.

Bentham was anxious to see the administration of the law put on a scientific footing. Punishment was to be seen as a kind of 'expense' both in terms of suffering to prisoners and in terms of the cost of keeping them. Its deterrent effects were a kind of 'income'. The object should be to obtain a maximum of 'income' at the least possible 'expense'. By this test certain cases will turn out to be ones where it will be 'unprofitable' to punish at all. These would include trivial offences but also those where punishment would cause great public hostility, upset relations with a foreign power, or in some other way do more harm than good. Again there were punishments that were severe out of all proportion to the seriousness of the offence. If effective deterrence could be achieved by a lesser sentence then, according to utilitarian principles, it is useless (a needless expense) to impose a higher sentence. Moreover, there was a fundamental problem about how to judge the seriousness of an offence. And this problem takes us to the heart of Bentham's dissatisfaction with the way the law was administered in his time.

In Bentham's time judges enjoyed great discretion in the punishments they could mete out. It was a matter of how serious *they* thought the offence was. But judges were recruited from the governing élite of Britain. They were likely to be particularly shocked at strongly-worded criticisms of persons in authority or by the then illegal 'conspiracies' of workers to try to force up their wages. Very severe punishments could be imposed for doing things which are no longer crimes at all. But even in matters where judges were not actually biassed, their judgements were inclined to be subjective, i.e. based on their feelings. For this reason Bentham rejected the appeal to 'conscience' and its philosophical variants such as the idea that we are possessed of a 'moral sense'. What was needed was for the administration of the criminal law to be guided by what Bentham called 'an external standard'. This 'external standard' was to be found in a science of human nature or what was then called 'moral science'. Indeed, Bentham thought that morality itself was founded on facts of human nature.

1.3 BENTHAM'S PRINCIPLES

Bentham's best known work is called *Introduction to the Principles of Morals and Legislation.* It was printed in 1780 though Bentham was hesitant about making its contents public and it was not published until 1789. Here is a short extract from the beginning of this work. You will find (I hope) that paragraphs (2)–(10) cover ground that is already partly familiar to you.

1 Nature has placed mankind under the governance of two sovereign masters, *pain* and *pleasure*. It is for them alone to point out what we ought to do, as well as to determine what we shall do. On the one hand the standard of right and wrong, on the other the chain of causes and effects, are fastened to their throne. They govern us in all

we do, in all we say, in all we think: every effort we can make to throw off our subjection, will serve but to demonstrate and confirm it. In words a man may pretend to abjure their empire: but in reality he will remain subject to it all the while. The *principle of utility* recognises this subjection, and assumes it for the foundation of that system, the object of which is to rear the fabric of felicity by the hands of reason and of law. Systems which attempt to question it, deal in sounds instead of sense, in caprice instead of reason, in darkness instead of light.

But enough of metaphor and declamation: it is not by such means that moral science is to be improved.

2   The principle of utility is the foundation of the present work: it will be proper therefore at the outset to give an explicit and determinate account of what is meant by it. By the principle of utility is meant that principle which approves or disapproves of every action whatsoever, according to the tendency which it appears to have to augment or diminish the happiness of the party whose interest is in question: or, what is the same thing in other words, to promote or to oppose that happiness. I say of every action whatsoever; and therefore not only of every action of a private individual, but of every measure of government.

3   By utility is meant that property in any object, whereby it tends to produce benefit, advantage, pleasure, good, or happiness, (all this in the present case comes to the same thing) or (what comes again to the same thing) to prevent the happening of mischief, pain, evil, or unhappiness to the party whose interest is considered: if that party be the community in general, then the happiness of the community: if a particular individual, then the happiness of that individual.

4   The interest of the community is one of the most general expressions that can occur in the phraseology of morals: no wonder that the meaning of it is often lost. When it has a meaning, it is this. The community is a fictitious *body*, composed of the individual persons who are considered as constituting as it were its *members*. The interest of the community then is, what? – the sum of the interests of the several members who compose it.

5   It is in vain to talk of the interest of the community, without understanding what is the interest of the individual. A thing is said to promote the interest, or to be *for* the interest, of an individual, when it tends to add to the sum total of his pleasures: or, what comes to the same thing, to diminish the sum total of his pains.

6   An action then may be said to be conformable to the principle of utility, or, for shortness sake, to utility, (meaning with respect to the community at large) when the tendency it has to augment the happiness of the community is greater than any it has to diminish it.

7   A measure of government (which is but a particular kind of action, performed by a particular person or persons) may be said to be conformable to or dictated by the principle of utility, when in like manner the tendency which it has to augment the happiness of the community is greater than any which it has to diminish it.

8   When an action, or in particular a measure of government, is supposed by a man to be conformable to the principle of utility, it may be convenient, for the purposes of discourse, to imagine a kind of law or dictate, called a law or dictate of utility: and to speak of the action in question, as being conformable to such law or dictate.

9   A man may be said to be a partisan of the principle of utility, when the approbation or disapprobation he annexes to any action, or to any measure, is determined by, and proportioned to the tendency which he conceives it to have to augment or to diminish the happiness of the community: or in other words, to its conformity or unconformity to the laws or dictates of utility.

10   Of an action that is conformable to the principle of utility, one may always say either that it is one that ought to be done, or at least that it is not one that ought not to be done. One may say also, that it is right it should be done; at least that it is not wrong it should be done: that it is a right action; at least that it is not a wrong action. When thus interpreted, the words *ought*, and *right* and *wrong*, and others of that stamp, have a meaning: when otherwise, they have none.

Exercise

1   What do you think Bentham means by saying that 'Nature has placed mankind under the governance of two sovereign masters, *pain* and *pleasure*'?

2   Why do you think Bentham says that 'every effort we can make to throw off our subjection [to these "sovereign masters"], will serve but to demonstrate and confirm' their sovereignty?

 Specimen answers

1   Bentham seems to have in mind two points. One is that human beings are naturally constituted so as to be drawn to what is pleasant and to shun what is painful. The other is that human beings naturally approve what gives rise to pleasure and disapprove what produces pain.

2   Bentham seems to be arguing that we cannot avoid being drawn to what is pleasant and shunning what is painful because that is how we are constituted. It is an inevitable fact of human nature. People who pretend it is otherwise, Bentham claims, only provide a confirmation, presumably because they still *seek* pleasure, only take pleasure in other things than what are usually thought of as 'the pleasures of life'.

 Discussion

Bentham held a view sometimes called 'psychological hedonism' – a view often put forward as if it stated a kind of scientific law about how people behave. ('Hedonism' is a word coined from the Greek word *hedone* which means 'pleasure'.) Human beings, it is suggested, 'gravitate' towards what is pleasant as surely as anything dropped from a height will gravitate to earth. So too they will be repelled by what is unpleasant or painful. This is claimed to be an unalterable fact of human nature. But there are, within limits, many differences in what individual people find pleasant or unpleasant. These differences arise from people's varying backgrounds and experiences, and not because they have chosen to be the way they are. Our actions, according to Bentham, spring from motives which, so to speak, are decided for us by the way in which we have been modified by our upbringing and environment. Bentham's view is what is called 'determinism' – a theory that you will be considering more fully later on. The sustained metaphor he uses in paragraph (1) suggests just this. Phrases like 'governance of two sovereign masters', 'fastened to their throne', 'subjection' and 'empire' suggest that we are subjected in our behaviour to forces over which we have no control.

 Exercise

Given what you know of Bentham's view about human nature, what do you think is implied about the prospects of human beings acting *morally*?

 Discussion

You may have thought that the prospects are not at all encouraging. It is often said, for instance, that morality is a matter of consideration *for others*. But if we are bound to seek our own pleasures, that suggests our primary concern is for ourselves, that our primary motive will be *self-interest*. Bentham accepted that this was, by and large, true:

> In every human breast, rare and short-lived ebullitions [outbursts], the result of some extraordinary strong stimulus or incitement excepted, self-regarding interest is predominant over social interest: each person's own individual interest, over the interests of all other persons taken together.
>
> In the few instances, if any, in which, throughout the whole tenour or the general tenour of his life, a person sacrifices his own individual interest to that of any other

person or persons, such person or persons will be a person or persons with whom he is connected by some domestic or other private and narrow tie of sympathy; not the whole number, or the majority of the whole number, of the individuals of which the political community to which he belongs is composed.

If in any political community there be any individuals by whom, for a constancy, the interests of all the other members put together are preferred to the interest composed of their own individual interest, and that of the few persons particularly connected with them, these public-spirited individuals will be so few... that to every practical purpose they may, without any practical error, be laid out of the account. (Bentham, *Works*, Vol. ii, p. 482)

 Exercise

Do you think Bentham can consistently allow that *anyone* sacrifices his own individual interest to those of other people? If so, how?

 Discussion

There is not much problem about the person who sacrifices his interest to someone 'with whom he is connected by some domestic or other private and narrow tie of sympathy'. For special ties of sympathy make the happiness of one person dependent to some degree on those of certain others. Sufficiently so that, consistently with the view of people Bentham gives us, we may expect there to be cases where an individual will sacrifice his individual interests for those of someone close to him. A mother may go without food herself rather than allow her children to starve. And so on.

The more problematic case is where there is no 'private and narrow tie of sympathy'. How, on a hedonistic account of human behaviour, is it possible to explain self-sacrifice in the interests of 'all the other members put together'? That is by no means clear. And yet, paradoxically, that is exactly what a utilitarian is called upon to approve. Consider paragraph (9) of the extract above.

A man may be said to be a partisan of the principle of utility, when the approbation or disapprobation he annexes to any action, or to any measure, is determined by, and proportioned to the tendency which he conceives it to have to augment or diminish the happiness of the community...

A *sincere* utilitarian would not simply *approve* the sacrifice of his own interest to that of the community as a whole but would presumably be *willing*, where the occasion demanded it, to make the sacrifice. Yet it seems as if Bentham is committed to claiming that it is virtually impossible to be a *sincere* utilitarian. He says, after all, that we can disregard, for practical purposes, those very rare people who do sacrifice their own interests for the general interest.

1.4   DIFFICULTIES IN BENTHAM'S PHILOSOPHY

Bentham seems to be caught in a dilemma: *either* psychological hedonism – the view that human beings are bound to seek what gives them pleasure and to avoid what causes them pain or distress – is false and it is possible for us to be utilitarians: *or* hedonism is true and there are no *sincere* utilitarians.

 Exercise

Can you see how Bentham might escape from this dilemma? (Spend only a few minutes on this question.)

 Discussion

Utilitarians might, as some have done, simply reject hedonism as a false account of human nature and substitute something else for it. They might offer a different psychology or no psychology at all. But if they offered no psychology at all then they could not claim that their theory was based on human nature. Bentham would not have accepted either of these options. For he held hedonism to be just that account of human nature which made utilitarianism plausible. That pleasure, happiness and so on were desirable neither had nor needed any proof. Bentham's claim is that we are so constituted that we cannot seriously dispute it.

Philosophers have traditionally talked much about dilemmas, as if the person confronted by a dilemma was like a defenceless matador confronted by a bull, in danger of being impaled on one horn of the dilemma or the other. Ways of escape include escaping between the horns, i.e. denying that one has to accept one or other of the alternatives: or grasping one or other of the horns, i.e. accepting one of the alternatives but denying that its consequences are quite so bad as the critic implies.

I have argued that Bentham cannot be expected to 'grasp' the first horn. His psychological hedonism was a basis for his utilitarianism. So he could not reject hedonism without cutting off the branch he is sitting on. What about escaping between the horns? This is a way out for some utilitarians, as we shall see later. It might be argued that human beings who are merely selfish cannot be really happy and hence that there is a pleasure to be found in helping others. But this is not a way out of the dilemma that fits with what Bentham says about the self-interested character of human conduct.

Bentham might, however, grasp the second 'horn' of the dilemma. He might accept that there are no *sincere* utilitarians (or as near to none as makes no difference). But, he might say, that does not really matter, from his point of view. He is not trying to improve human nature, he might say, but rather to alter the social 'fabric' in such a way that society could be happier even with human nature as it (inevitably) is.

 Exercise

Bentham's *Introduction to the Principles of Morals and Legislation* is mostly concerned with the reform of the criminal law and the penal system. This is perhaps the most striking example of what he had in mind when he said that his aim is 'to rear the fabric of felicity by the hands of reason and law' (paragraph (1)). What do you think such reform has to do with getting people to act morally?

 Discussion

The answer I was fishing for is that one main purpose of the criminal law is to curtail the pursuit of self-interest where this involves doing harm to others. An effective system of law will deter most people from serious harm to others (theft, grievous bodily harm, slander, and so on) by their fear of the harm (punishment) that might come to them if they did.

In order to induce people to act morally, according to Bentham, it is necessary to have 'sanctions'. As well as the sanction of the law, Bentham allows what we would call a 'social' and he called a *'popular'* sanction. Our behaviour is modified because we desire the approval of others and wish to avoid their disapproval. Bentham allows a 'religious' sanction, in which he included the hope of heaven and the fear of hell, though this sanction would only be effective in the case of people with firm religious convictions. These sanctions between them constrain human behaviour insofar as it is constrained.

Bentham's concern was primarily with what he called the 'political' sanction, the sanction of the criminal law. He wanted to see the law reformed so that, for instance, there were legal sanctions only against actions that were 'wrong' by utilitarian principles. But, since such sanctions could only be effective by deterring people from committing crime, it was necessary for the law to be clear, the prospect of punishment to be as nearly certain as possible, and so on. Moreover, since punishment is in itself a harm, it should be no more than is necessary to deter others from committing the same crime.

1.5   BENTHAM'S INFLUENCE

I have sketched Bentham's approach in broad terms but have failed to give you any sense of the meticulous detail in which he spelt out the reforms he wanted. He was not just concerned, as I have been, with general principles. Bentham not only favoured the ballot, but prescribed the exact specifications of a ballot box. He not only wanted a more efficient prison service but drew detailed diagrams of the lay-out of prisons. Above all, however, he was able, as a trained lawyer, to put forward his proposals for reform of the criminal law in the kind of detail needed for parliamentary legislation.

Bentham was not short of admirers. But neither was he short of critics. Utilitarianism came to be much criticized, even hated, by a substantial body of influential men. This was not just because it was radical and anti-religious, nor even (though there was much anti-French sentiment in early nineteenth-century Britain) because of its debt to French thinking. Nor was it only because Bentham's hedonism seemed to many to involve a depraved view of human beings – though his stress on the motives of self-interest and pleasure did arouse much moral indignation. It was also because Bentham's followers, in becoming a political sect, became identified with various policies that were seen by the poor (and the small number of middle-class people like Charles Dickens who cared about the lot of the poor) as both oppressive and inhuman. How this came about and how much these criticisms bear on utilitarianism as such, are matters we shall discuss in the next section.

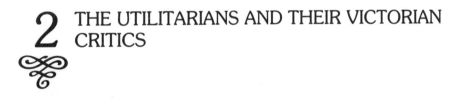

2   THE UTILITARIANS AND THEIR VICTORIAN CRITICS

2.1   JAMES MILL AND 'THE PHILOSOPHICAL RADICALS'

The fame and influence of Jeremy Bentham was largely due to his writings. Bentham was something of a recluse – not, by temperament, the kind of person who would gather disciples round him. Though Bentham's writings were the main inspiration for the British utilitarians in the early nineteenth century, their leader was James Mill (1773–1836). James Mill, the son of Scottish shoemaker, could afford to go to Edinburgh University, thanks to one Sir John Stuart. I mention this John Stuart since James Mill gave this name, doubtless as an expression of gratitude, to his son. John Stuart Mill was to become more famous than his father and it is John Stuart Mill's classic restatement of utilitarianism that we will be looking at in the next section. But James Mill's contribution to the development of utilitarianism was a very important one. In the first place he brought to it a greater breadth of knowledge than Bentham, in particular of psychology, education and political economy. Moreover, it was James Mill who managed to form around him a group of very able men, some of whom became Members of Parliament, who came to be known as 'the Philosophical Radicals'.

James Mill himself was a civil servant (as was his son for much of his life) and therefore could neither stand for political office nor be too much involved in political agitation. Nonetheless he was the leader of the group that included a number of men of distinction such as the economist David Ricardo, the historian George Grote and the jurist John Austin. In the early decades of the nineteenth century they were instrumental in securing a number of reforms that favoured the underprivileged classes. They were obsessed with the thought that what was needed above all was a constitutional safeguard against 'the sinister interest' of the governing classes, something they believed could only be achieved by extending the right to vote and by secret ballots. The 1832 Reform Act went some way in the direction they wanted, adding a large number of middle-class and a small number of working-class men to the electorate. The Philosophical Radicals believed that this new electorate would provide them with the base on which they could become a major political party. But they were mistaken. 1832 was a turning point in their political fortunes, but in the other direction from what they had hoped. The 'Philosophical Radicals' became what was no more than a 'left wing' of the then Whig Party. By the 1860s, when John Stuart Mill was an MP, they thought of themselves as 'advanced' (i.e. progressive) liberals.

2.2   THOMAS GRADGRIND AS A 'PHILOSOPHICAL RADICAL'

It seems that Dickens intended Thomas Gradgrind, MP for Coketown in *Hard Times,* as a parody of a 'Philosophical Radical'. This has been disputed, on the ground that Gradgrind's system of education cannot be connected with historical utilitarianism. And it is Gradgrind as an educationalist who occupies such a central place in *Hard Times.* His politics are of marginal relevance. Nonetheless his politics clearly are those of a Philosophical Radical. When Dickens mentions that 'the Gradgrind party' was in some way opposed to 'fine gentlemen' (p. 164) he is almost certainly satirizing the obsession of Bentham's followers with curtailing 'the sinister interest' of the aristocracy. This is confirmed by Dickens's reference on the same page to their 'little mouldy rations of political economy' for, as we shall see, the Philosophical Radicals had been enthusiasts for this new science. One of their intellectual heroes had been Adam Smith, after whom one of Gradgrind's sons is named. Again, the calculating Bitzer, when Gradgrind is tempted to appeal to him not to betray young Tom Gradgrind, throws Gradgrind's philosophy back in his face with this remark:

> I am sure you know that the whole social system is a question of self-interest. What you must always appeal to, is a person's self-interest. It's your only hold. We are so constituted... (Dickens, *Hard Times,* p. 383)

This remark is clearly directed against Bentham's utilitarianism. Gradgrind, almost on the point of appealing to Bitzer's better nature (in case he had one), changes tack and asks him his price.

The final twist to this little scene lies in Bitzer's remark: 'I was brought up in that catechism when I was very young, sir, as you are aware'. Bitzer had, of course, been at Gradgrind's school. Earlier it had seemed that Gradgrind's school simply taught rather meaningless facts to no obvious purpose. But now it seems that part of its purpose was to indoctrinate pupils with utilitarian ideas. What Dickens seems to have done is to present Coketown as a place where religion was curiously lacking in influence, but where its place was largely taken by utilitarianism. Gradgrind's system, as David Craig points out in his introduction to the Penguin edition (pp. 22 ff.), is very similar to the Bell and Lancaster systems which were quite influential in Dickens's time. These systems were ones that would serve the purposes of religious indoctrination well. But there was a rivalry between them, with one having the support mainly of Anglicans and the other having the support of freethinkers and others, including some of the utilitarians. Although there is no factual basis for the Gradgrind school it is evidently a portrayal of what Dickens imagined a utilitarian school might be like.

Philosophers familiar with the writings of Bentham and the Mills have found it difficult to recognize that Dickens was satirizing utilitarianism. Their difficulty is understandable. For Dickens was attacking a very decadent form of utilitarianism in which the cardinal point, i.e. the connection with the greatest *happiness* of the greatest number, is somehow forgotten in favour of an obsession with numbers for their own sake. The utilitarian enthusiasm for basing social decisions on facts is truncated to an interest in facts and statistics for their own sake. And so on. This could hardly have been a mistake or misunderstanding on Dickens's part. I think Gradgrind was deliberately represented as someone busily going through the motions of being a scientific reformer but who had lost sight of the point of what he was doing. That would hardly have been fair comment on Bentham and the Mills. But it may be fair comment on the impression which the utilitarian MPs made in virtue of their stances on particular social issues.

2.3 THE UTILITARIANS AND THE LABOURING POOR

A central social question of the time was poverty. The utilitarians were, of course, concerned with the remedies for poverty but their theories and the measures they approved came to seem hard-hearted. Three aspects of their policies are particularly important:

1 They followed Adam Smith in thinking that the problem should be dealt with by policies that would allow the rich to become richer. The argument for this is a very complicated one and occupied a good part of Smith's *Wealth of Nations* (1786) but it was very influential on nineteenth-century 'political economy'. Roughly, Smith's argument was that the only way for a wealthy person to become wealthier was to invest his money in productive work. The increase in work available would lead to an increase in competition for labour and this in turn would make it necessary for employers to pay higher wages, thus raising the standard of living of even the poorest.

2 This optimistic view was, however, brought in question by the arguments of Thomas Malthus in his *Essay on the Principle of Population* (1798). Malthus claimed that the population was bound to increase much faster than the means of supporting it and that the only checks on the growth of population were such things as war or famine. Thus Malthus (after whom another of Gradgrind's sons was named) revealed a serious snag in Smith's theory. Had there been effective means of birth control the utilitarians might have advocated their widespread use. But that was not an option at the time. Accordingly, the utilitarians took the view that the labouring poor ought to be taught that sexual abstinence was in their own interests.

3 In 1832, a Royal Commission was set up to investigate the problem of 'pauperism' in England and Wales and the ways in which local provision was made for the relief of the poor. A dedicated utilitarian, Edwin Chadwick, was a leading figure on this body and it is the work of the Commissioners and Assistant Commissioners that (fairly or unfairly) gave utilitarians their public image of a group obsessed with facts and figures. Dickens's reference to 'commissioners of fact, who will force the people to be a people of fact' (p. 9) is probably an allusion to utilitarians like Chadwick. At all events the Poor Law Report of 1834 condemned the existing arrangements as encouraging idleness and dependence and proposed changes that would make it in the interest of the destitute to do all they could to fend for themselves and their families. The report proposed that all those who were destitute be required to enter workhouses where they would indeed be kept from starving but where they would be subject to a regime as unpleasant as a prison.

The rationale behind the new arrangements was not purely utilitarian. Leading Victorians were very committed to hard work and to the virtues of self-reliance and were attracted by a punitive view of the idle poor. But the new arrangements could be given a utilitarian justification. Hard labour is something humans will naturally avoid, according to Bentham's hedonistic psychology. If, therefore, it is in the interest of the community that people should work hard and fend for themselves, they need to be provided with the incentive to do this. For this purpose the workhouses would need to be places nobody would go to, unless in desperation.

The Poor Law Reforms were enforced in the south of England but so great was the agitation against them in the north that they were never enforced throughout the country. The utilitarians backed these 'reforms' and perhaps this, more than any other political stance they took, gave them the image of hard-hearted oppressors of the poor and put paid to any prospect they might have had of becoming the party of the underprivileged.

2.4   UTILITARIANISM IN 'HARD TIMES'

The Gradgrind party in *Hard Times* is a parody of the utilitarians and is presented as a party in disarray, forced to seek support wherever they could find it, including amongst 'fine gentlemen' like James Harthouse. 'There never before was seen on earth such a wonderful hybrid race as was thus produced' is Dickens's damning observation on page 164.

On the back cover of the Penguin edition of *Hard Times* there is the following claim:

> In the persons of Gradgrind and Bounderby he [Dickens] powerfully stigmatized the prevalent philosophy of Utilitarianism which, whether in school or factory, allowed human beings to be caged in a dreary scenery of brick terraces and foul chimneys, to be enslaved to machines, and reduced to numbers.

 Exercise

In the light of what you have read so far in these units, and of your earlier work on *Hard Times,* how true do you think this statement is?

 Discussion

The statement blames the main evils of industrialization on the existence of utilitarianism as 'the prevalent philosophy', as if these evils would not otherwise have persisted. This, to begin with, involves a fantastic exaggeration of the importance of utilitarianism, not only in fact but in Dickens's estimation. If utilitarianism had been that prevalent then Gradgrind would not only have been Prime Minister but the head of a one-party state. On the contrary, it seems to me, Coketown is one of the last footholds of a party on its way out and Gradgrind's influence a very peculiar feature of the place. But in any case Gradgrind is only to blame for the school, not the housing or the conditions of work in the factories. These are largely to be blamed on Bounderby. Yet Bounderby says nothing whatever that could associate him with the philosophy of utilitarianism. I take the point of the Bounderby connection, like that with James Harthouse, to have to do with the compromises necessary to the pursuit of political power. Without the support of men like Bounderby the likes of Gradgrind would never have been returned to Parliament.

Gradgrind is, however, to blame for the education of his children and for the products of his school. An important part of the novel consists in his reaping the unhappy harvest from the educational seeds he has sown – the failure of his daughter Louisa's marriage, the moral shortcomings and eventual ruin of his son Tom and, as I mentioned earlier, the calculating Bitzer who cares nothing at all for the welfare of anyone else. But, as we have seen, this application of utilitarianism is original to Gradgrind. The image of utilitarianism is of a philosophy which has failed. The Gradgrind party were 'exhausted' (p. 157) and clearly on the way out. Gradgrind himself comes to realize the inadequacy of his educational theory and by implication of utilitarianism. After all there is 'a wisdom of the Heart' as well as 'a wisdom of the head' (p. 246). There is a place for feeling as well as reason.

The 'blurb' on the back cover of the Penguin edition of *Hard Times* makes it seem as if utilitarianism dominated Britain in rather the way in which, at the time of writing, Khomeini's Islam dominates contemporary Iran. Quite the contrary, I believe. Dickens's message is a political one. Utilitarianism was a spent force and could not be looked to as a way of improving the condition of the people. Dickens indeed portrays all the 'Radicals' in a poor light, including the trades unionists. What he seems to be favouring instead is a humane Conservatism.

Dickens once had a job that required him to sit through and take detailed notes of the debates at the House of Commons. This was at the very time (early 1830s) when Mill had concluded that the Philosophical Radicals were on the decline. Mill thought that the Radical MPs were poor representatives of the utilitarian cause. They needed a leader who would 'put ideas into their heads, and purpose into their hearts' (*Autobiography*, p. 113). For a while Mill did what he could to rally them but without success. The Radicals became a 'left wing' of another party and it is this compromised and demoralized band that Dickens caricatures in *Hard Times*.

2.5   DICKENS AND EARLIER CRITICISMS OF THE UTILITARIANS

Dickens seems, for the reasons I have just given, to have regarded utilitarianism as a *symptom* rather than the cause of the sicknesses of his time. That was the view of Thomas Carlyle, to whom *Hard Times* was inscribed. In 1829 Carlyle had written an influential article called 'Signs of the Times' in which he diagnosed 'this age of ours' as 'the Mechanical Age'. Carlyle did not simply mean that his age was

Figure 2   Thomas Carlyle (1795–1881). A leading social critic of the early Victorian period. Amongst his best-known works were The French Revolution *(1837),* Chartism *(1839),* On Heroes, Hero-worship, and the Heroic in History *(1841), and* Past and Present *(1843). (Photo: Illustrated London News, February, 1881)*

increasingly marked by the use of machinery in factories, though that was indeed quite true. His main point was that men 'are grown mechanical in head and heart, as well as in hand'. As Carlyle explains:

> Not the external and physical alone is now managed by machinery, but the internal and spiritual also. Here too nothing follows its spontaneous course, nothing is left to be accomplished by old natural methods. Everything has its cunningly devised implements, its pre-established apparatus; it is not done by hand, but by machinery. Thus we have machines for Education: Lancastrian machines; Hamiltonian machines; monitors, maps and emblems. Instruction ... is no longer an indefinable tentative process, requiring a study of individual aptitudes, and a perpetual variation of means and methods, to attain the same ends; but a secure, universal, straightforward business ...'

Carlyle linked this with many other symptoms of the mechanical tendency, including utilitarianism which, with its emphasis on constitutional reforms as the solution to the main problem of 'the sinister interest', seemed to Carlyle to be bent on mechanistic solutions.

Echoes of Carlyle's ideas are everywhere in *Hard Times,* including his emphasis on individual energy, imagination and spontaneity, all of which are embodied in the circus people who symbolize an alternative and more humane culture in contrast with that which predominates in Coketown. Nothing indeed is more characteristic of the dominant culture of Coketown than the regime of its school as described in the early chapters of *Hard Times* – which was modelled on the Lancastrian system, according to the editor of the Penguin edition (pp.22–3). Utilitarianism is only one aspect of this dominant culture – by no means the root cause of the problem but not any kind of solution to it either. That, I believe, is the view shared by Carlyle and Dickens.

The burden of these criticisms was already familiar to the utilitarians back in the 1820s. At least they were, if John Stuart Mill's *Autobiography* is to be relied upon. Curiously, Mill himself went through a mental crisis which brought him to the verge of losing faith in utilitarianism. He came to think that in his youth he himself was for a while a 'mere reasoning machine' and that the charge commonly levelled against the followers of Bentham was one which 'though extremely inapplicable to most of those who have been designated by that title ['Benthamite'], was during two or three years of my life not altogether untrue of me'. Mill went on to note other common criticisms:

> Utility was denounced as cold calculation; political economy as hard-hearted; anti-population doctrines as contrary to the natural feelings of mankind. We retorted by the word 'sentimentality' ...

Mill was certainly brought up to regard feelings with suspicion, as were the Gradgrind children. But at least after his crisis of faith, Mill came to think very differently about feelings and about the imagination and came to the view that a satisfactory education would cultivate them. When he came to formulating his own version of utilitarianism he took account of the criticisms made by Carlyle and others, as we shall see in the next section.

Two of these criticisms may be highlighted now, since they are in a way implicit in *Hard Times.* One is that, because it took the production of pleasure to be the object of morality, utilitarianism was in Carlyle's words a 'pig philosophy'. The phrase 'pig philosophy' was intended to capture the complaint that utilitarianism licensed the pursuit of 'pleasure' in a narrow sense, that is the pursuit of sensual or what the Victorians called 'lower' pleasures. In *Hard Times* this criticism is embodied in the way in which the Gradgrind regime provided young Tom Gradgrind with no defence against the debauching influence of James Harthouse.

The other criticism is one we noted earlier – that Bentham's philosophy takes human beings as basically self-interested in their behaviour and therefore, especially if the fear of hell-fire is removed, there is a problem as to what 'sanction' there is against those whose behaviour is immoral but not illegal. The Gradgrind school produced the repulsive Bitzer, whose moral education had not left him with any interest except in the welfare of 'number one'. Mill believed that utilitarianism could be stated in such a way as to be free from these objections. In an indirect way, then, Mill can be taken as offering a reply to the criticisms which Dickens thought put paid to utilitarianism as a serious philosophy. We shall consider shortly whether he succeeded or not.

3 JOHN STUART MILL'S 'UTILITARIANISM'

In this section we shall be looking at Mill's statement of utilitarianism and his defence of it against two charges, in particular: (a) that utilitarianism is a 'pig philosophy', unable to give greater weight to higher values than the pursuit of the pleasures of sense; and (b) that utilitarianism seems to make it all right for people to be treated unfairly or unjustly. Mill's *Utilitarianism* (1863) is an extended essay that deals with other problems as well. But the two we shall be concerned with were certainly thought by Mill to be important.

Before dealing with the first of these objections Mill found it necessary to say something about an 'absurd ... misconception' as to what utilitarianism is. That is what Mill is concerned with in the first of the two opening paragraphs of the extract in the Appendix to these units 'What Utilitarianism Is' (pp. 78–9).

 Exercise

Read these two paragraphs now. When you have done so, answer the following questions.

1   In what sense, according to Mill, was the word, 'utilitarian' most 'popularly' known?
2   What misunderstanding, according to Mill, did the existence of this 'popular' sense of the word 'utilitarian' cause amongst critics of the philosophical school known as 'the Utilitarians'?

 Discussion

1   In the most 'popular' sense, the word 'utilitarian' was applied where pleasure was rejected or neglected, for example, to things that were functional rather than ornamental.

2   The misunderstanding caused by extending this popular use of the word to the philosophical school known as 'the Utilitarians' was that of taking them to reject pleasure in favour of something else whereas, as Mill brings out in the second paragraph, the tendency to produce pleasure or happiness was for the utilitarians the very criterion by which an action was to be judged right. So, far from neglecting it, the utilitarians put pleasure at the centre of their moral theory.

Mill represents this misunderstanding as an 'ignorant blunder' but this, I think, is hardly fair to the critics of utilitarianism. The utilitarians had, after all, been champions of a more cost-effective prison service and a harsh system of poor relief. They had also preached sexual abstinence in those without the means to support families. And even if they have said that the whole point of such austerities was the greatest happiness of the greatest number (in the long run), it is at least understandable that the critics should have failed to see that this was the point and to suppose rather that the point was to protect the pockets of the rich. The *Morning Herald* (3 September, 1839) condemned what it called 'the cold "philosophy" of a money-getting utilitarian age' and, if it made a 'blunder' as to what utilitarianism was, it was not as baseless and 'ignorant' as Mill would have liked to think.

In the circumstances Mill might have done well to abandon the word 'utilitarianism' entirely. In a footnote he explains that he did indeed abandon it for a while but that he decided to retain it because of a 'want in the language' of any other term to refer to the set of opinions he wished to defend. That is such a feeble reason that it is difficult to believe it to be the whole story. In fact, Mill had adopted the word 'utilitarian' for the Benthamite group which he led as a young man, abandoned the label during a period of revolt against Bentham's ideas, and

Figure 3 John Stuart Mill (1806–1873). Leading British philosopher of the mid-nineteenth century. His System of Logic *(1843) and* Principles of Political Economy *(1849) were much used as textbooks. His* On Liberty *(1859),* Representative Government *(1861),* Utilitarianism *(1863) and (The* Subjection of Women *(1869) are still widely regarded as classics. (Photo:* Illustrated London News, *March, 1866)*

came back to it in what he describes in his *Autobiography* as the 'third period' of his 'mental progress' in which he claims, 'I . . . completely turned back from what there had been of excess in my reaction against Benthamism'. In retaining the word 'utilitarianism', Mill was not just using one word for want of a better but identifying himself positively once more with the Benthamite tradition in which he had been brought up. For this reason the work is on the defensive right from the start. Having dismissed the 'popular' misunderstanding of utilitarianism Mill turns almost immediately to what he regards as a more serious charge, namely, that utilitarianism is a debased philosophy, unable to give priority to the finer qualities of human life.

3.1   MILL ON 'HIGHER' AND 'LOWER' PLEASURES

Mill is concerned in *Utilitarianism* to defend a moral point of view with a tradition stretching 'from Epicurus to Bentham'. Epicurus (*c.* 341–*c.* 270 BC) was an important philosopher of ancient Athens who taught that the universe is basically material, that our knowledge of it is only through the senses, that there is no hereafter and hence that our happiness is to be sought in this life and there is no reason to fear what will happen to us after we die. In spite of the fact that Epicurus taught that happiness is to be found in virtue and in simple living, his teachings were popularly understood as if he valued sensual pleasures above all other. And, indeed, the word 'epicurean' is commonly used of someone who is partial to the orgiastic pleasures. In the rest of the extract 'What Utilitarianism Is' Mill attempts to defend Epicurus and the utilitarians against the charge that they advocated a 'pig philosophy'.

 Exercise

Read the rest of that extract (Appendix, pp. 64–7) now. When you have done so, please make a note of your answers to these questions:

1   How, according to Mill, are 'higher' pleasures to be distinguished from 'lower' ones?

2   How satisfactory do you think Mill's distinction is?

Discussion

1   Mill thinks that people who experience the same pleasures will largely agree as to which are the more desirable (and therefore 'higher') and that the question as to which of two pleasures is higher should be referred to 'the judgement of those who are qualified by knowledge of both'. If they do not agree, he adds, the judgement 'of the majority of them, must be admitted as final'.

2   There are many different ways of responding to this question and I may not have anticipated yours. But, in the first place, comparing pleasures is not like being a judge at a cat show. Each of the panel of judges at a cat show is expected to rate the cats by broadly the same criteria as the other judges and to judge the next cat show by the same standards. But people find the same things more or less pleasant and the same person will find the same thing more or less pleasant on different occasions. Worse still, no one would expect a panel of experts to judge whether a cat was better than a cucumber. Yet this is the kind of exercise in which Mill's panel of judges would need to engage, comparing unlike with unlike.

It might seem that Mill need not insist on agreements about the ranking of pleasures to make his point. And indeed, if his only object were to distinguish human pleasures from those of a pig, it would be enough to point to the greater complexity of human pleasures. (It could even be allowed that pigs are a bit more complicated than Mill supposes.) But there is a further problem about not being able to rank pleasures. It is that, without such a ranking, the project of trying to produce the greatest happiness of the greatest number becomes a nebulous one.

3.2   THE PROBLEM OF MEASURING HAPPINESS

Mill's project of grading pleasures according to quality was an attempt to preserve the moral theory he had been brought up with in the face of the objection that some pleasures are more desirable than others. Bentham seems to have imagined that happiness was something like wealth that might be measured in one way or in another. We can talk meaningfully about how wealthy an individual is because we can measure this in money terms. This is not, of course, a wholly problem-free exercise since it is not just a matter of adding a bank-balance to cash in hand. But if a price can be put on someone's assets, say, in terms of what they would be worth if 'realized' at a particular time, a figure would be produced which would provide a measure of how wealthy that person was at that time. But obviously someone who was worth £30,000 at 1925 values would have been much wealthier than someone who was worth that sum in 1975. In order to make the comparison it is necessary to adopt some arbitrary date and talk in terms of pounds at, say, their 1975 value. It would then be possible to ask questions like 'Were doctors better off in 1925 than they were in 1975?' and even 'Is the population as a whole better off now than they were in 1975?', 'Are the poor becoming poorer?', and so on.

This comparison with wealth is of particular relevance, since utilitarians have tended to talk as though there was a 'sum of human happiness' to be increased or diminished, as if happiness was a kind of wealth and misery a kind of poverty. Supposing, for a moment, that this is true, there is a further problem for utilitarians. For they seem to be committed to saying that what matters morally is the gross amount, and not how it is distributed. Just as the total amount of wealth in a society might increase, even though the poor became poorer, so the total amount of happiness might increase even though those who were deprived were suffering greater deprivations. The utilitarian seems committed to saying that this is an improvement from a moral point of view. Whereas it would seem, on the contrary, to be the opposite. It seems, that is to say, morally objectionable that the deprived should be further deprived even if at the same time those who are relatively advantaged are made proportionately happier than are the others made more miserable. It is morally objectionable because it is *unfair*.

Exercise

How do you think a utilitarian might reply to this objection?

 Discussion

A utilitarian might, of course, deny that questions of fairness (of a fair distribution of happiness) mattered. But most of us (I think) would agree that they do matter and so if the objection is not taken seriously utilitarianism will seem to us to that extent an unattractive theory. That would be too high a price to pay for not bothering with such objections. And Mill, it is worth noting, devoted about a third of his *Utilitarianism* to a chapter on a related issue, 'On the Connection between Justice and Utility'.

The most plausible line of reply I can think of, on the utilitarian's behalf, is to say that the example is an unreal one. 'In reality', he might say, 'you cannot increase the total sum of happiness by making lives that are already pleasant more pleasant at the expense of those who are deprived. The increased misery of the deprived will always weigh in the balance more than any increased happiness. Unfairness always involves a violation of the "greatest happiness" principle and so is always wrong.' Such a reply would be along the lines of Mill's utilitarian explanation of why it is we ought to treat people *justly,* i.e. it tries to show how 'unfairness' is not a separate moral consideration but that, on the contrary, the moral force of considerations to do with fairness is actually explained by utilitarianism.

You can see how this argument, like most philosophical arguments, could go on for a long time. There is sure to be more that could be said in defence of utilitarianism in reply to my objection that it licenses unfairness. (You may have thought of different replies to the one I said was 'the most plausible I can think of'.) But here are two observations that I would like to make in the light of that reply.

1   My utilitarian claimed that cases of unfairness are always violations of 'the greatest happiness principle' and so wrong for that reason. But to know this we would need to have some proper way of measuring happiness. Yet even if there was some as yet undetected vibration inside us (like purring in cats) which increased in proportion to our sense of pleasure it would still not provide us with what we need. We should also need a measure of distress that could be calibrated on the same scale. Moreover, we would still be left with problems over more complex pleasures, such as I hope you are deriving from studying this course. (Even cats seem to derive pleasure from various kinds of play activity, such as chasing balls of wool, but do not appear to purr and perhaps do nor purr at all on these occasions.) In the absence of any means of measuring happiness, talk of increasing the sum of human happiness is very nebulous and there is no way of telling whether or not all cases of unfairness will be cases where the total sum of human happiness has been diminished.

2   Mill's distinction between 'higher' and 'lower' pleasures would, if it worked, only add to the problem. For it would license giving an additional weighting to the 'higher pleasures'. If access to these (going to the opera, for instance) turned out to be increased by material wealth, then it could well be that, on Mill's criteria, it would be right to redistribute wealth in favour of the better off. On the other hand, if there is no sensible way of grading pleasures, the introduction of considerations to do with the quality of pleasures only serves to make talk of the 'sum of human happiness' even more nebulous.

That is not a conclusive objection to utilitarianism and I hope you thought there might be more to be said in the utilitarian's defence. After all, it is not uncommon for people to want to leave the world a better place than they found it, and although this is rather vague it does not mean that no one has ever failed or succeeded. The objections I made only throw in doubt the project of deciding what is right and wrong with scientific precision in every case. And they are only objections to certain forms of utilitarianism. Yet they are serious objections. Some utilitarian judges at one time thought that the beneficial consequences (deterrent value) of hanging those who were convicted of stealing sheep outweighed the harm done to the thief. Nowadays an educated Muslim might defend (I recently heard one do so) the practice of cutting off hands or feet of thieves as a terrible but effective way of halting the kind of crime wave all too familiar in the western world. Even if there were agreement as to the facts (what the deterrent value of a particular penalty would be) there is no way of putting the quantity of suffering caused and the quantity of suffering prevented into the balance so as to decide whether a particular penalty was justified.

3.3   UTILITARIANISM AS A SOCIAL PHILOSOPHY

We have been considering problems that arise for the utilitarian assumption that happiness can be measured and therefore that we can talk about increasing the amount of happiness. But these problems do not arise in every case. Frequently we do not need to imagine we have a measure of the suffering or pleasure and can simply suppose it is the same for each person. In these cases it is simply a matter of counting heads. If an action costs three lives but saves nine, then the action seems clearly to be right by utilitarian standards – so long as we can disregard differences between the individuals concerned and do not allow ourselves to be diverted by the thought that some lives might be more worth saving than others. Again it may even be possible to take account of objective differences between individuals. A surgeon is likely to choose a younger patient to receive an organ transplant rather than an older one on the ground that the younger person is more likely to recover and in any case has a greater 'expectation of life'. His argument is a utilitarian one. Though he is not, strictly, increasing happiness – simply securing for a longer time what in a phrase of Mill's might be called 'the means of happiness'.

These considerations suggest a direction in which we might go in restating utilitarianism. We could do this by claiming that all human beings have certain needs and that, if these needs are met, and for as long as they are met, they are provided with 'means of happiness'. That is not to say that people will be happy if all their needs are met or that they cannot be happy unless they are. A beggar, it has often been observed, can be happier than a king. But in general such a utilitarian would have to say that people are not able to be happy if, for example, they lack adequate food, shelter or clothing or if they are ill, lonely or bored. People's needs are not all equally basic and the priorities among them may not be wholly agreed. But, from the utilitarian's point of view, the virtue of talking in terms of human needs is that it makes some sort of sense to talk of maximizing happiness, namely, maximizing the number of people who have 'the means of happiness', i.e. whose basic needs are met.

We shall consider this way of reformulating utilitarianism later, in Section 5.3. It is only one of many ways of restating it. I will conclude this part of our discussion by drawing your attention to two core features of utilitarian theories. One is that they regard actions as right and wrong solely in virtue of their likely consequences and therefore, since the likely consequences of an action are a question of fact, utilitarianism makes questions of right and wrong turn on the facts. For a utilitarian, for example, the question whether the state is right to inflict capital punishment on murderers will depend on whether the consequences of having the death penalty deters would-be murderers. And that people are deterred would be expected to show itself in a reduction in the number of murders – a question of fact. The other core feature of utilitarian theories is that they make out actions to be right in virtue of maximizing something (happiness, the means of happiness, or whatever). This feature has the consequence that governments, since they have much more power, are much more important as moral agents than are individuals.

These features partially explain the fact that the utilitarians were much interested in what Bentham knew as 'moral science' (social sciences, psychology, penology, etc.) and also that they looked to political action to achieve their ideals. These features also explain, perhaps, why utilitarianism should have become a dominant moral theory in the public arena without also becoming, as Mill hoped, a kind of successor to religion. For utilitarians make issues turn, so far as possible, on objective facts rather than individual conscience. It also gives a special moral importance to public agencies. Mill did not foresee this result and indeed looked to co-operation between individuals rather than government intervention as the means of social improvement. Like most of the Victorians, as you will find in later units, Mill regarded government intervention in society with suspicion. We, by contrast, mostly think that governments have a positive moral duty to intervene to secure to all citizens some of the basic 'means of happiness'. The Education Act of 1870, with its aim of providing a minimal education for all, was a milestone along the road that led eventually to the complex health and welfare provisions of the post-1945 period.

In the light of these developments it is not difficult to understand why some have wanted to say that utilitarianism is really about *social* morality and not about *personal* morality at all. The utilitarian seems bound to say that it matters much more morally what governments and powerful social groups do precisely because more happiness is at stake with their actions. The ordinary person has very little power for good or ill and to that extent his choices are relatively trivial, from a utilitarian point of view. We will consider this further in the next section.

4 UTILITARIANISM, CONSCIENCE AND PERSONAL MORALITY

The idea that personal morality is centrally a matter for conscience has long been and still remains one that many find if difficult to resist. But conscience is also, and has long been, a highly problematic notion. Bentham had gone so far as virtually to deny it altogether. He thought those who took themselves to be guided by the promptings of an inner moral sense were only misled by their feelings. And in any case, according to Bentham, human beings are primarily motivated by self-interest. Conscience, on this view, is both unreliable and impotent.

Mill agreed with Bentham on the unreliability of conscience. Moral feelings, according to Mill, are acquired and can be cultivated in almost any direction, 'so that there is hardly anything so absurd or so mischievous that it may not . . . be able to act on the human mind with all the authority of conscience' (*Utilitarianism*). On the other hand, Mill thought that, given the right moral education, people could be made more co-operative, more concerned with the welfare of others. As we shall see later (Units 20–21), Mill thought that the type of society in which he lived produced people in whom self-interest was predominant. Mill would have agreed with Dickens that Bitzer is indeed the product of a very defective moral education in a bad social environment. Mill does not, unlike Bentham, suppose that human beings are naturally self-seeking rather than altruistic, but believes they are capable of being either, depending on the character fostered by social institutions and upbringing.

Mill certainly wanted his utilitarianism to provide an underpinning for personal morality. Indeed, he claimed that 'no reason has ever been shown why [the conscientious feelings of mankind] may not be cultivated to as great an intensity in connection with the utilitarian, as with any other rule of morals' (*Utilitarianism*).

He seems to have thought, moreover, that utilitarianism was an ethic that could be shared equally by the Christian and the non-religious person. He thought of utilitarianism as the ethics of Jesus of Nazareth without the specifically religious beliefs attached to it. But, although utilitarianism was independent of religion, it was not, he frequently stressed, hostile to it. He rejected the charge that utilitarianism was essentially a '*godless* doctrine', claiming that 'whatever aid religion, either natural or revealed, can afford to ethical investigation, is as open to the utilitarian moralist as any other' (*Utilitarianism*).

It is evident from this that Mill, while he took on the mantle of his father as the leading champion of utilitarianism of his generation, was anxious to present utilitarianism as a way of thinking his contemporaries need not find alien. On the one hand he sought not to compromise what he saw as essential to the utilitarian point of view. On the other hand he sought to accommodate as many features of ordinary moral thinking as he could. In this spirit he does not deny the connection between conscience and personal morality, but only certain theories as to the nature of conscience.

4.1   CHAMPIONS AND GUARDIANS

The theories that Mill attacked with special zeal were those of what he called the 'intuitional school' of philosophy. According to this school all true knowledge (including knowledge of right and wrong) is founded on truths that are grasped by the intellect. Such truths are recognized immediately or intuitively, hence no reason can be given why they are true. In this sense of the word 'intuitive' certain basic truths of mathematics were supposed to be 'intuitive': for example $1 + 1 = 2$. What these philosophers thought was that certain basic moral truths were 'intuitive' in the same way. Mill by contrast identified himself with a quite different 'school' (usually known as 'empiricism') according to which all true knowledge is based on experience.

Mill thought the distinction between these two 'schools of philosophy' was of fundamental significance, for reasons he explains in his *Autobiography*. This comes out particularly in a passage that tells of his activities in the 1860s:

> Now, the difference between these two schools of philosophy, that of Intuition and that of Experience and Association, is not a mere matter of abstract speculation; it is full of practical consequences, and lies at the foundation of all the greatest differences of practical opinion in an age of progress. The practical reformer has continually to demand that changes be made in things which are supported by powerful and widely-spread feelings, or to question the apparent necessity and indefeasibleness of established facts; and it is often an indispensable part of his argument to show how these powerful feelings had their origin, and how those facts came to seem necessary and indefeasible. There is therefore a natural hostility between him and a philosophy which discourages the explanation of feelings and moral facts by circumstances and association, and prefers to treat them as ultimate elements of human nature; a philosophy which is addicted to holding up favourite doctrines as intuitive truths, and deems intuition to be the voice of Nature and of God, speaking with an authority higher than that of our reason. In particular, I have long felt that the prevailing tendency to regard all the marked distinctions of human character as innate, and in the main indelible, and to ignore the irresistible proofs that by far the greater part of those differences, whether between individuals, races, or sexes, are such as not only might but naturally would be produced by differences in circumstances, is one of the chief hindrances to the rational treatment of great social questions, and one of the greatest stumbling-blocks to human improvement. This tendency has its source in the intuitional metaphysics which characterized the reaction of the nineteenth century against the eighteenth, and it is a tendency so agreeable to human indolence, as well as to conservative interests generally, that, unless attacked at the very root, it is sure to be carried to even a greater length than is really justified by the more moderate forms of the intuitional philosophy. That philosophy, not always in its moderate forms, had ruled the thought of Europe for the greater part of a century.

Exercise

1   What view of conscience does Mill attribute, by implication, to the school 'of Intuition'?

2   Why did Mill think it so important to oppose this school?

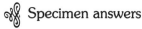 Specimen answers

1   Mill does not use the word 'conscience' in this passage but it is clear that the faculty of 'intuition' performs the role of conscience. It is supposed to be 'the voice of Nature and of God, speaking with an authority higher than reason'. It is 'innate', 'indelible' and one of the 'ultimate elements of human nature', not to be explained in terms of 'circumstances and association'.

2   Mill evidently saw the school of Intuition as an obstacle to progress. At bottom, adherents of this school were guardians of 'conservative interests'. They were 'addicted to holding up favourite doctrines as intuitive truths' and so engaged in defending prejudices as 'necessary and indefeasible' facts. Mill alludes specifically to prejudices as to the 'innate' differences between races or the sexes.

 Discussion

You may have been slightly puzzled by Mill's stress on the word 'association'. The psychological theory Mill accepted put great stress on a process known as 'association of ideas' and is commonly known for that reason as Associationism. This theory is explained in Part II of these units so I will not enlarge on it now. Sufficient to observe that Mill took it for granted that a progressive moral philosophy would be based on the sciences of man and that these sciences would be founded on experience. Science, reform and utilitarianism were all inter-connected so far as Mill was concerned. The 'intuitional philosophy', by contrast, 'discourages the explanation of feelings and moral facts by circumstances and association' and it is 'one of the greatest stumbling-blocks to human improvement'. It is, in short, anti-scientific and reactionary, in his view.

These claims by Mill need, of course, to be taken with more than a grain of salt. He had a very simplified and partisan view of the history of philosophy. Those whom Mill lumps together as forming the intuitional school of philosophy are a much more varied group of people than he implies and by no means all of them can be fairly charged with being anti-scientific and reactionary. The passage we have just looked at does, however, serve to suggest to us how Mills' career as a politician, moralist and reformer is linked with his career as a writer on more abstract matters. At least two of his books (his *System of Logic* and his *Examination of Sir William Hamilton's Philosophy*) were expressly directed against the intuitional philosophy.

There is more to be said for utilitarianism than some of its nineteenth-century critics allowed. But there is also more to be said for the intuitional view of ethics than Mill allowed. And indeed it often happens in philosophy that it is useful, in order to get a critical perspective on the view with which we are mainly concerned, to look at an opposing view. We may in this way be able to see better where the strengths and weaknesses of each way of thinking lie. Let us then look at the intuitional alternative to utilitarianism.

4.2   INTUITIONALISM AS AN ALTERNATIVE MORAL THEORY

I have already suggested that intuitional theories are actually much more diverse than Mill supposes. We do not have time to delve back into earlier philosophy in order to see this variety. So we will not be able to consider whether Mill was fair in charging the intuitionalists with 'holding up favourite doctrines as intuitive truths' and, as it were, seeking to promote their own prejudices as though they had all the authority of mathematics. My opinion is that they sometimes did but that then they were not being as rigorous as they should. Yet they need not have done. The charge that intuitionalism is *always and necessarily* an appeal to something subjective is, in particular, one that does not stand up to close scrutiny.

Let us look at intuitionalism in a form that is in one way very strong and in another way rather modest. A moral intuitionalist may make this claim:

> There are some moral facts that are known with all the certainty of the basic truths of arithmetic.

Here are some examples of what such an intuitionalist may claim to be moral facts:

1   We should be loyal to our friends.
2   We should pay our debts.
3   Only the wrong-doer should be punished.

That these are facts is something we grasp by 'intuition', it may be claimed. What is meant by this is that we immediately see these statements to be true once we have fully grasped their meaning. Just as no one who understood what is meant by the statement '2 + 3 = 5' could doubt that it is true, so no one who could fully understand what is meant by the statement 'We should be loyal to our friends' can doubt whether it is true.

If someone is unconvinced of this then what is needed is an analysis of the statement in question. For instance, in the case of '2 + 3 = 5' we can start by defining '5' as '4 + 1', '4' as '3 + 1', '3' as '2 + 1' and '2' as '1 + 1' and proceed by various stages to substitute definitions for the symbols they define until we have identical symbols on either side of the 'equals' sign:

1   3 + 2 = 5
2   3 + 2 = 4 + 1
3   3 + 2 = (3 + 1) + 1
4   3 + 2 = 3 + (1 + 1)
5   3 + 2 = 3 + 2

In this 'proof' of '3 + 2 = 5' I have been doing things with brackets. In logic and mathematics there are very strict rules about what you are allowed to do with brackets. A fully rigorous proof would appeal to these rules and would explain at each step exactly how it followed the previous one. But what I have done will, I hope, be sufficient to show how such an analysis might go.

It is not possible to analyse moral statements with anything like the same rigour. All the same it is possible to bring out the connection between being a friend and being someone to whom loyalty is owed. This might be done by drawing attention to the use of the phrases 'true friend' and 'false friend'. A true friend is someone who stands by us in our hour of need. ('A friend in need is a friend in deed.') A false friend is one who deserts us when the going ceases to be smooth.

The first of the moral facts I listed connects with the second. Loyalty is something we *owe* to our friends. It is, we might say, the *price* of friendship. Hence we can speak of a 'debt of loyalty'. When we speak of debts we think, of course, primarily of money and you may have reservations about conceding that it is true that we ought to pay our debts. If so, you may, in a way, be quite right since our legal 'debts' and our moral 'debts' may not be the same. Suppose for instance someone borrows money at an exorbitant but none the less legal rate of interest. Such a person may be legally required to pay a debt that far exceeds anything that would be morally just. To avoid this complication the intuitionalist needs to say that we legally ought to pay our lawful debts and we morally ought to pay our 'moral' debts. Suppose that I rush off to work one day and find, when I have arrived that I do not have the price of a cup of coffee (have left my cheque book, etc. behind) and borrow a small amount from a colleague. Such a debt might not be recoverable by legal process but it is a debt all the same and one I am morally bound to pay.

Exercise

Try doing your own analysis of the third 'moral fact' I offered as one that we know as certainly as the truths of arithmetic. That was 'Only the wrong doer should be punished.' (Look up 'punishment' in a good dictionary if you are foxed by this exercise.)

 Discussion

A dictionary definition of 'punishment' is likely to say something like 'penalty inflicted on an offender'. As in our previous example it is possible for legal and moral cases to come apart. Someone may legally be punished for an offence that no one thinks is morally wrong. But if they did not commit the offence they ought not to have been penalized. That the (legally) innocent cannot (legally) be punished is a matter of what we mean by 'punishment'. So we could not describe what a parent was doing as 'punishing' a child without supposing the parent to believe the child to have done something wrong. If the belief is mistaken (e.g. some other child did the wrong) then the punishment was unjustified.

Intuitionalism, as I have stated it, is not going to serve us as a comprehensive moral theory. To defend it in this form is not to defend the way of thinking about morality as obeying the dictates of the inner voice of conscience that the utilitarians were particularly concerned to oppose. It does not tell us that we should help those in need, and not one of the Ten Commandments is a moral fact in this sense. All the same it may serve to provide some contrast with a utilitarian theory. For if there are any moral facts of this kind there are moral truths that we know in a way the utilitarian cannot allow. The utilitarian holds that whether or not something is right or wrong depends *entirely* on its consequences. According to intuitionalism we know that we ought to do certain things and not do others independently of consequences. According to the intuitionalist, being disloyal to our friends is something that is wrong in *itself*. So too is failing to honour a debt and punishing people who are innocent. But the utilitarian holds – and must hold – that no action is right or wrong in *itself*. So, according to the intuitionalist, the utilitarian is mistaken.

4.3   UTILITARIANISM ON THE DEFENSIVE

 Exercise

How do you think utilitarians might respond to this challenge?

 Discussion

There are many ways in which they might respond. Here are two of them.

1   They might say that although it is indeed 'obvious' that we should be loyal to our friends (and so forth), this is no more than a generalization. It is, it might be said, true *as a rule*. Moreover, it is true *as a rule* for utilitarian kinds of reason, that is, because being loyal to our friends (and so forth) is found as a rule to promote human happiness. This is something that is confirmed by human experience.

2   They might say that in any case there is nothing 'absolute' about such obligations as loyalty. They can be overridden in particular circumstances and then it would be apparent that utilitarian considerations are the ones that count. Supposing, for instance, you arrange one morning to give a friend a lift to work but at the last minute you learn that someone else urgently needs taking to hospital. No one else is available with transport. We would all think that the right thing to do was to take the sick person to hospital. The fact that this person might be a total stranger would not affect the matter. So it is sometimes right to let your friends down.

Exercise

Do you think these are satisfactory answers?

 Discussion

1   As it stands, I do not think that it is satisfactory to claim that 'We should be loyal to our friends' is a *generalization*. That is because friendship is partly constituted by obligations of loyalty. It is part of what is meant by saying that one person is a 'friend' of another that they are bound together by such obligations. So it is implausible to claim that it is a generalization for the same reason that it would be implausible to claim (as Mill, incidentally, did) that arithmetical truths are generalizations.

2   The other point the utilitarian might make about obligations that we allegedly know we have independently of experience is that they are not in any case 'absolute' obligations. They can be overridden in a variety of circumstances. Utilitarians can readily agree that it is wrong to be disloyal to a friend. Friendship, they may say, is itself a source of happiness and therefore anything that might tend to break it would, other things being equal, be wrong because it would be wrong to put a friendship in jeopardy. But, a utilitarian would say, other things are not always equal. It may be necessary, in particular circumstances, to choose between letting down a friend and a worse evil, say, refusing to go to the aid of someone injured in an accident. The right thing to do in cases of moral conflict will often be a matter of doing the lesser of two evils, according to utilitarianism.

So far this seems a satisfactory line of answer. Few of us would imagine that the obligation to honour a promise to a friend to give him a lift to work was 'absolute' in the sense that nothing could excuse failure to carry it out. But we may be uneasy about the utilitarian's apparent willingness to deny the absolute character of any moral obligation. We might be worried because we think there are some things it would be wrong to do in any circumstances. We might think, for example, that it is quite wrong to kill an innocent person and wrong irrespective of the circumstances. They may be sure that in nearly all circumstances it would indeed be wrong. But they must be willing to consider each case on its merits. It might be argued, for instance, that it is right to kill an innocent person if this is the means of saving the lives of many innocent persons. The utilitarian cannot reasonably refuse to be drawn into such an argument. And this leads to the suspicion that utilitarianism is a corrupt philosophy that might be used to licence almost anything.

As we have seen, utilitarianism was already being severely criticized in the nineteenth century, and John Stuart Mill, who accepted some of the criticisms, found himself having to reformulate the theory. It is indeed characteristic of philosophical theories that they undergo this process of revision in the light of criticism. Debates about them often go on for centuries, as has been true of both the theories we are discussing in this 'Introduction to Philosophy'. Particular precise formulations of such theories can, effectively, be proved wrong. But the theories themselves are more likely to die out than actually be refuted. It may come about that, for a variety of reasons, no one is inclined to defend a theory any more. That is the fate that seems to have befallen what Mill attacked as 'Intuitionalism'. But other theories show a remarkable resilience in spite of being beset by criticisms. Those who are still tempted to defend them, if they are ingenious enough, seem always to be able to find another way of doing so. For these reasons such theories have been aptly likened by one modern philosopher (Sir Geoffrey Warnock) to citadels under siege – 'much shot at perhaps but never taken by storm, which are quietly discovered one day to be no longer inhabited' (Warnock, p. 11). The two theories we are concerned with in these units – utilitarianism and determinism – may be described in terms of this metaphor as citadels that were 'inhabited' in the nineteenth century and are still inhabited today.

This is not to say that philosophical discussion is carried on nowadays in much the same way as it was by the Victorians. On the contrary, in common with many other subjects that existed in the Victorian period, philosophy has changed a great deal. In the concluding section of this part of the units I shall indicate some of the major changes that affect the modern debate about utilitarianism. You will be returning to John Stuart Mill and Victorian philosophy in the course of your study of Units 16–32. But, in the meantime, we shall be concerned for the rest of these units with modern approaches to the subject.

5   UTILITARIANISM AND PHILOSOPHY TODAY

5.1   PHILOSOPHY IN THE TWENTIETH CENTURY

There are a number of respects in which philosophy as practised today in universities is importantly different from what it was like in Mill's time. One of the most obvious differences is that the scope of the subject is no longer as broad. Philosophy had been a kind of 'super-subject' concerned to bring together the results of all the special sciences so as to arrive at an overall view of the world. Philosophy had been 'the queen of the sciences'. Even in the nineteenth century, by which time the natural sciences were pursued largely independently of philosophy, philosophy was still the master-subject so far as the human sciences were concerned. The subject known as 'moral philosophy' or 'moral science' has been taken to include every kind of study of human nature. The economist Adam Smith had been Professor of Moral Philosophy at the University of Glasgow. Jeremy Bentham's *Introduction to the Principles of Morals and Legislation* was intended (see Section 1.3 above) as a contribution to what he thought of as 'moral science'. Mill's father wrote a book on psychology and Mill himself wrote an important book called *Principles of Political Economy* as well as contributing to the subject now known as 'sociology'. Psychology and economics were still being taught in universities under the auspices of philosophy departments well into this century. Cambridge still retains the old title 'Moral Sciences' for its philosophy department. The older Scottish universities all had, at least until recently, departments of 'moral philosophy'. But, in spite of what these old titles imply, the sciences of human nature have for some years invariably been taught in specialist departments of psychology, economics, sociology and so on.

Philosophy has, in a way, lost an 'empire' as the social sciences have become disciplines in their own right and its identity, like their's, has accordingly changed a good deal. Amongst the many changes that have taken place, there is one you might have been led to expect from my earlier remarks about the centrality of argument in serious philosophy. The study of argument, also known as logic, has developed into a highly complex and technical subject in the twentieth century, partly thanks to a modern philosopher you are likely to have heard of, Bertrand Russell.

There are few philosophers who are content to say that philosophy should consist only of logic. In the tradition of logical analysis the task of philosophy has been taken to be to analyse concepts or to establish such truths as can be discovered by the analysis of concepts. This may sound a strange process but we have already discussed examples of such 'analytic' truths (statements that are true in virtue of the meanings of the terms they contain) in Section 4.2 above, such as

'2 + 3 = 5' or, though this is an example by no means as obvious, 'We should be loyal to our friends'. This is not to say that such logical analysis offers support to the intuitionalists. For, as I suggested in Section 4.2, the truths that they can hold onto turn out to be rather less numerous or substantial than the intuitionalists believed. Intuitionalists regarded themselves as guardians of moral truth, as having on the authority of reason a role to play not unlike that the clergy perform on the authority of the Bible or the Church. In the 1930s, leaders of the analytical movement in philosophy, like Gilbert Ryle, tended to repudiate the role of 'missionary' (Ryle's phrase) and to insist, as indeed academics were increasingly doing in all disciplines, on their professionalism.

5.2   MODERN MORAL PHILOSOPHY

Modern philosophers differ not only from the intuitionalist philosophers of the eighteenth and nineteenth centuries but also from John Stuart Mill in the following respect. Mill and the intuitionalists shared the belief that there was some kind of absolute basis for moral judgements. They disagreed about what it was, of course, but this disagreement does not by itself appear to have undermined their confidence that such a basis existed. The intuitionalists thought there were some actions that were self-evidently right in themselves or wrong in themselves (see Section 4.2 above) without reference to their consequences. And an 'intuition', in this sense, is a kind of immediate awareness that something is true. Such 'intuitions' form the basis of our moral judgements, according to that theory. But in most moral matters there is nothing self-evident about the judgements we make. If an attempt is made to rely upon 'intuition' in most cases it appears to become an appeal to something subjective. So if I say I have an 'intuition' that it is right to turn the other cheek or wrong to eat meat I am telling you something about me, something subjective. And this is different from when I say that I have seen the train go by, in which case I am telling you something 'objective' and not just about me, namely, that the train has gone by.

I am not saying that when someone says 'You ought not to eat meat', 'You ought to turn the other cheek', and so on, they are saying something 'subjective', though some people have said that too. What I am saying is that when someone says 'I have an intuition that you ought not to eat meat' (and so on) they are saying something subjective. The point is about the word 'intuition', which has changed its meaning so that to our ears it signals something merely subjective. So, far from providing a basis for the judgement 'You ought not to eat meat', an appeal to intuition seems to suggest it is a matter of nothing more than individual feelings.

Bentham and Mill wanted to escape from reliance on anything like intuition and to offer an 'external standard' of right and wrong. In Mill's case, as we saw in Section 3.1, he hoped to be able to grade the higher pleasures on the basis of the verdicts of connoisseurs, as if everyone would agree on such matters given the same experiences of them. But, as we saw in Section 3.2, there seems no sensible way of reaching agreement as to which is the better of two very different pleasures. Mill was in danger, in the event, of seeking to impose in the name of higher pleasures, the subjective preferences of an elite group of people like-minded with himself. So Mill's utilitarianism seems, in the end, to lead to subjectivity as much as does intuitionalism.

Partly because of the kinds of difficulty such rival moral theories have encountered there has been a tendency in twentieth-century philosophy to deny that there is any universal basis for moral judgements. This has commonly been expressed by saying that there are no moral truths in the sense in which there are truths discovered in science. That the moon goes round the earth, that the continent of Australia was once joined to South America, that the dodo is now extinct, all these are 'objective' truths about the world. Even if we were not quite sure whether they are true, what we would be uncertain about is none the less something true or false independently of us. It is in this sense that philosophers have denied that there are objective moral 'truths'.

It would not, however, follow from this that there is no place for reasoning in moral matters. For, after all, it may turn out that those who take part in discussions of moral matters do, by and large, react in similar ways to moral situations. This is sometimes expressed by saying that we do, by and large, often have the same moral 'intuitions', the word 'intuition' now being used to mean something subjective, as 'hunch' is about matters of fact. Our moral intuitions are not a *basis* on which moral theory can be built since they include feelings that may conflict with one another and which, therefore, may need to be modified in the light of further reflection. But they provide points from which philosophical discussion of moral matters can start and to which moral theories like utilitarianism need to return.

For these reasons examples have become very important to modern moral philosophy. The favoured method of discrediting a moral theory is to find a 'counter-example', i.e. to find an example where the theorist is committed to saying one thing but we are strongly inclined to say the opposite. Those who argue against utilitarianism, such as Bernard Williams (see television programme 13), adopt such strategies. They produce counter-examples that have the effect, if they are successful, of making us aware of respects in which utilitarianism conflicts with our moral intuitions. Our moral intuitions might, of course, be changed on reflection. But the argument of such critics as Williams is that, rather than become utilitarian in our feelings about moral matters, we should look for a moral theory that does better justice to the moral intuitions we have.

There are certain features of utilitarianism that may sound all right in the abstract but which, when considered in terms of examples, we are likely to see as counter to our intuitions. The utilitarian, for instance, is committed to denying that any action is right or wrong in itself and to saying that the rightness or wrongness of an action derives entirely from its (likely) consequences. A philosopher might try to think of a 'counter-example' where it is plausible to say that something is wrong in spite of leading to better consequences all round. Here is one example devised by Bernard Williams:

> Jim finds himself in the central square of a small South American town. Tied up against the wall are a row of twenty Indians, most terrified, a few defiant, in front of them several armed men in uniform. A heavy man in a sweat-stained khaki shirt turns out to be the captain in charge and, after a good deal of questioning of Jim which establishes that he got there by accident while on a botanical expedition, explains that the Indians are a random group of the inhabitants who, after recent acts of protest against the government, are just about to be killed to remind other possible protesters of the advantages of not protesting. However, since Jim is an honoured visitor from another land, the captain is happy to offer him a guest's privilege of killing one of the Indians himself. If Jim accepts, then as a special mark of the occasion, the other Indians will be let off. Of course, if Jim refuses, then there is no special occasion, and Pedro here will do what he was about to do when Jim arrived, and kill them all. Jim, with some desperate recollection of schoolboy fiction, wonders whether if he got hold of a gun, he could hold the captain, Pedro and the rest of the soldiers to threat, but it is quite clear from the set-up that nothing of that kind is going to work: any attempt at that sort of thing will mean that all the Indians will be killed, and himself. The men against the wall, and the other villagers, understand the situation, and are obviously begging him to accept. What should be do?

 Exercise

Think about the above example. What advice would a utilitarian give to Jim as to what he should do? Do you regard this as obviously the right answer?

⚜ Discussion

The utilitarian should advise Jim to kill the one Indian so as to save the lives of the others. But, and this was Williams's point in proposing the example, we might feel that it would not be mere squeamishness on Jim's part if he refused to do it. It might seem morally the right thing to do even though another nineteen lives are lost as well. Why? Williams suggests that it is because, while Jim is not responsible for the situation he is in, he is specially responsible for what he himself does. Williams suggests that the value we attach to how we conduct ourselves, independently of questions to do with the overall situation and the effects of our actions on overall outcomes, is closely connected with the value of integrity. The purpose of the example is rhetorical. It is intended to bring home to us an implication of utilitarianism we may not like. But of course you may have thought, and may still be thinking, that the utilitarian's advice is the right one. There is no single moral intuition that is the right one to have in this case.

John Stuart Mill did not make use of examples in this way but he was clearly aware that there were areas of difficulty for utilitarianism, as previously formulated. As we saw he devoted a large chapter to discussing one of those areas – justice. Some of the problems connected with this topic – such as whether it is ever right to punish someone who is innocent – will be discussed further at the end of Part II. In the meantime let us return to an earlier objection and consider whether utilitarianism can be reformulated so as to meet it.

5.3   RESTATING UTILITARIANISM

I have already suggested that a theory like utilitarianism admits of many different formulations and is more likely to run out of defenders than it is to be refuted. In television programme 13 Bernard Williams puts forward a number of reasons for thinking that utilitarianism is too 'thin' a moral theory, that it cannot accommodate the wide range of things we think intuitively are morally important. Integrity and loyalty might be included amongst the non-utilitarian virtues. But, though these are serious objections, it may be possible for utilitarians to revise their theory so that it is less obviously open to the objection of being excessively narrow. Mill was certainly trying to do this in arguing that the utilitarian can explain why justice is important.

Let us look at another case. Williams has argued that one defect of utilitarianism is that it cannot explain the priority we give to meeting people's needs *over* gratifying their whims. As a consequence, he argues (in television programme 13), the utilitarian seems committed to making what appear intuitively to be morally wicked choices. Given the choice between meeting the basic needs of a few and the whims of the overwhelming majority, it seems that the utilitarian would find it hard to avoid having to say that the whims of the overwhelming majority should be gratified. But intuitively we may feel that gratifying people's whims, no matter how many people are involved, can never be a moral priority. And I would be inclined to go further and say that they have no moral claim on us at all. By contrast, the fact that there are people whose basic needs are not met, supposing we are in a position to help them, does give them a moral claim on us. Or so it might appear.

It might seem that if such a radical objection were accepted then utilitarianism would need to be rejected. But it would be possible to reformulate what could still be recognized as a highly modified form of utilitarianism, namely, the one I introduced in Section 3.3. According to this view, we do not have a general obligation to create as much happiness as possible but to secure to as many people as possible 'the means of happiness'. In this form, utilitarianism is not concerned with maximizing happiness all round. In the language of wage-negotiators, it is 'bottom-loaded', i.e. it concentrates benefits on those who are worse off, those whose needs are not met and who therefore are, it is supposed, denied 'the means of happiness'.

Bottom-loaded utilitarianism is a reformulation that meets a number of the common objections to utilitarianism. In particular it recognizes the greater moral claim on us of people in need. But of course it does so at a price, namely, of having nothing to say about our moral obligations to those who are not in need. And yet it seems clear that we can have obligations towards them, for instance, by making promises to them. This so-called bottom-loaded utilitarianism provides an account of how we have obligations to people with whom we have no connection. But it fails to explain the kinds of obligation we think we have to friends, family and people with whom we acquire special relationships (e.g. by making them promises). At best, then, it offers only a partial explanation of why we have the obligations we think we have.

This last criticism is related to one of the most persistent objections to utilitarianism, that it is in the end not a personal morality at all but a public morality. Utilitarianism has a built-in assumption that every person counts equally and this makes it seem that any special obligation we may think we have to look after our own children rather than others that equally need looking after is a kind of bias. Again, with its stress on consequences, utilitarianism seems bound to attach more moral significance to the actions of governments and agencies whose decisions have much more effect than to those of private citizens. These difficulties apply equally to bottom-loaded as to other forms of utilitarianism.

Utilitarianism remains an important moral theory and indeed is perhaps still the dominant moral theory in the public domain. Those concerned with medical welfare, for instance, will very commonly make use of utilitarian reasoning. It is also invoked in discussions about the treatment of offenders. We have touched briefly in this first part of these units on the justification of punishment. But this is a topic about which you will have an opportunity to think further towards the end of you study of Part II.

REFERENCES AND FURTHER READING

Bentham, J. (1982; first published in 1789) *An Introduction to the Principles of Morals and Legislation*, edited by J. H. Burns and H. L. A. Hart, Methuen.

Bentham, J. (1838–43 edn) *The Works of Jeremy Bentham*, edited by J. Bowring, Edinburgh, W. Tait; London, Simpkin Marshall & Co.

Carlyle, T. (1829) 'Signs of the Times', *Edinburgh Review*, Vol. XLIX, pp. 441–4.

Checkland, S. G. and E. O. A. (eds) (1974; first published in 1834) *The Poor Law Report of 1834*, Penguin.

Dickens, C. (1854) *Hard Times*, Penguin English Library edn, 1969 and Oxford University Press, 1989.

Golby, J. (ed.) (1986) *Culture and Society in Britain 1850–1890: a source book of contemporary writings*, Oxford University Press (referred to in the text as the Course Reader).

Halevy, E. (1928) *The Growth of Philosophic Radicalism*, translated by Mary Morris, Faber and Gwyer.

Helvétius, C.-A. (1758) *De l'Esprit*, published in London (1759) with the subtitle *Essays on the Mind and Its Several Faculties*.

Malthus, T. R. (1798) *An Essay on the Principle of Population*, J. Johnson.

Mill, J. S. (1863) *Utilitarianism*, many editions.

Mill, J. S. (1873) *Autobiography*, many editions.

Monroe, D. H. (ed.) (1972) *A guide to the British Moralists*, Collins.

Ryan, A. (1970) *The Philosophy of John Stuart Mill*, Macmillan.

Smart, J. J. C. and Williams, B. (1973) *Utilitarianism: For and Against*, Cambridge University Press.

Warnock, G. (1958) *English Philosophy Since 1900*, Oxford University Press.

Williams, B. (1972) *Morality: an Introduction to Ethics*, Cambridge University Press.

PART II   FREE WILL AND DETERMINISM

INTRODUCTION

This second part of the Introduction to Philosophy is about the problem of free will. The problem itself is quite distinct from those of ethics, but there are nevertheless a great many similarities and connections between the two subjects, which make them particularly suitable for studying together. Both, for instance, concern issues familiar to everyone, and not at all the special preserve of professional philosophers. They are discussed in ordinary situations, and most people have opinions about them. They are also both subjects with important practical consequences: the opinions people have about them considerably affect their attitudes to themselves and their activities, to the treatment of other people, and to public policy. They are also closely connected in other ways, some of which will appear in the course of the discussion.

Nevertheless, in spite of these similarities, the approach taken here will be quite different from the approach to the problems of ethics in Part I, in both style and pace. There you were introduced to the problems of ethics and the theory of utilitarianism through a historical study of the philosophers who first systematized the ideas, and through various contemporary and modern criticisms of their theories. Here, in contrast, there will be no history, and no study of the theories and texts of particular philosophical writers. Instead, the text takes the problem of free will simply as a problem in its own right, and plunges straight into a philosophical argument leading to a particular set of conclusions.

The idea behind this approach is to provide not only an introduction to the problem of free will, but also more sense of what it is to engage in a sustained philosophical argument than was possible in the space available in Part I. This is important, because the ability to follow and criticize sustained arguments, and to produce such arguments yourself, is essential to the study of philosophy. Although I do think the line of argument presented is broadly correct, and I hope you will find it persuasive, the purpose of the text is not to offer the ultimate solution to the problem of free will. (It should anyway be said that the conclusion I reach here is not the one I expected to reach when I started writing, and for all I know new arguments may later persuade me to revise this one.) The purpose is to introduce you to the problem, to illustrate various philosophical techniques, and to make you engage in philosophical argument.

The main problem with this kind of approach is that the argument does tend to rush along to its conclusions like a non-stop train, whizzing past dozens of stations where other philosophers (and you) might want to get off and change lines. This is inevitable in a text of this length: we cannot possibly stop to discuss all the objections that might be raised as the argument progresses. However, this is not a total disadvantage, because it provides an opportunity to practise the critical thinking essential in philosophy. If as you go along you find yourself suspecting that something is going wrong with the argument you should be ready to try to work out what it is, and then make sure that your own alternative line of argument stands up to criticism. This is all part of doing philosophy, so if you find it happening you should regard it as progress, rather than as an indication that the text has nothing to offer you.

Read, then, slowly and carefully. Make sure you understand the details of the argument (especially as it develops and gets more complicated) but at the same time try to keep in mind an overall view of the problem and the stage the argument has reached. The recapitulatory exercises at the end of each section should help you to do this. If you find from them that you have misunderstood what has gone on, read the section again and make sure you understand it before going on. And, as I said before, if you find the argument races past places where you would like to get off the train and explore branch lines, or at least sit on the platform and think, make a note of them for when you have time to make a more leisurely journey. It will probably be best to go straight through this text without many pauses at least in the first instance, if only to find out where the argument is going and how it gets there, but after that you can retrace your steps and stop as often as you want to. The further reading at the end will help to suggest other directions in which you might explore.

1 THE PROBLEM

1.1 ONE APPROACH TO THE PROBLEM

We normally think of ourselves as autonomous agents, capable of making free choices, able to influence the course of events by those choices, fully responsible for the choices we make, and deserving of praise or blame according to what they are. The philosophical problem of free will is of whether or not we are justified in holding these beliefs about ourselves.

Most of the time we take these beliefs for granted without a second thought. They are essential to our self image, and closely bound up with our attitudes to our lives and our opinions about how we and other people should be treated. But even though they may normally be taken for granted there are in fact all kinds of difficulties about them. These keep out of sight most of the time, but really they are lurking only just below the surface of our familiar habits of thought, ready in all kinds of circumstances to reach out and pull us towards the depths of a very murky underworld. In ordinary life, when practical problems are pressing on all sides and there is limited time for struggling in philosophical quagmires, it is usually necessary to draw back as soon as we feel ourselves being pulled into difficulties that present radical threats to the way we think. However, it is a philosopher's business to follow such difficulties wherever they lead, even if (as in this case) there is a danger of never being able to return to ordinary ways of thinking. The problem of free will may be at the familiar end of the spectrum of philosophical problems, but it is in many ways one of the most difficult and most thoroughly philosophical problems of all.

To see how easy it is to run into problems about freedom of the will, consider the following situation. It is imaginary in detail, but you will immediately recognize its roots in fact.

Suppose that after a night of considerable incident the courts of some small town find themselves having to deal with several serious cases of domestic assault. Most of these cases look quite straightforward, but two of them have turned out to present particular difficulty. One involves a husband who tried to strangle his wife; the other a wife who went for her husband with a kitchen knife. There is no doubt about the main facts in either case: both assaults were deliberate, and neither was in self defence. In each case, however, the court's resident psychologist has uncovered interesting evidence which seems to provide the basis of strong pleas in mitigation. In the first case it turns out that the man was conscripted during a recent war, put through intensive training designed to condition him to attack on the slightest provocation, and then plunged straight into combat. Before that time his character had been quite different, and violence had been completely alien to him. In the second case it turns out that the woman was at the time suffering from unusually severe pre-menstrual tension, and that at other times of the month she is known to everyone as a model of calm and restraint.

 Exercise

Imagine you are the counsel for the defence in these two cases, trying to persuade the judge to exempt the defendants from punishment, or at least to give them lighter sentences than the other people involved in the night's violence. How might you argue? (Remember, by the way, that the question here is specifically about punishment: a penalty for criminal activity. You may have to agree that your clients should be prevented from doing harm in future by being confined to institutions or by being given medical treatment, but your concern here is only to argue that *punishment* is inappropriate.)

 Discussion

Your argument might go something like this. 'We have good scientific evidence, in general', you might say to the judge, 'that such things as conditioning and hormones can influence character and behaviour. We also have particular evidence, already accepted by the court, that such influences were at work in these two cases. We know that the man was subjected to military training and war, and that before then his character was quite different. We know that the woman was suffering at the time of the attack from a hormonal imbalance, and that when there is no such imbalance her behaviour is beyond reproach.

'Now, neither of my clients had any control whatever over these influences that changed their characters. The man was conscripted against his will, the woman did not choose her hormonal constitution. They cannot therefore be held responsible for them. But *these influences were the cause of their violent behaviour,* and since my clients were not responsible for the *cause* of their behaviour, they were obviously not responsible for the behaviour itself. Since it is a basic principle of justice that people should not be punished for what they cannot help, it follows that it would be quite unjust to punish them. At the very least they should be punished less severely than all these other people who have no such excuses.'

This seems an entirely plausible line of argument. It is by now impossible to deny that physical constitution and training of various sorts have at the very least some influence on character and behaviour, and we have particularly good evidence in the case of such matters as war and pre-menstrual tension. However, you can probably see already where all this is leading.

 Exercise

Suppose the judge has accepted that these two defendants were not responsible for their actions and therefore should not be punished, and suppose now that you are the defending counsel for the rest of the people who have come up before the court. How might you argue for leniency on behalf of your clients?

 Discussion

You argument might go like this. 'You have decided', you might say to the judge, 'that if an action can be explained by environmental influences, such as military training, the defendant is not to blame for it. You have decided that the same thing applies when the action can be explained by such physical facts about the defendant as hormonal imbalances. And of course you are quite right. The defendants were not responsible for these things, and therefore were not responsible either for the crimes that resulted from them.

'Well, consider the rest of my clients. Here, for instance, is a woman brought up in a violent family, where she was never taught to control her temper. If she had been brought up differently she would have acted quite differently and would not have committed this crime. She obviously has to be let off for the same reason as the soldier. And here is another of my clients. He suffers from a chromosomal abnormality, but for which he would certainly not have been violent. He clearly has to be let off too.

'And in fact similar arguments apply to the cases of all these defendants, however normal their backgrounds and physical constitutions may seem to be. *All* my clients are the products of their physical make up (hormones and the like) and their environment, and those factors – all entirely beyond their control – provide the explanation of all their actions. Here, for instance, is an intelligent woman of excellent education and impeccable family background who tried to murder her husband just because she wanted to take his money and go off with her lover. She may seem to have no excuse at all, but she can no more help being the kind of character she is than the others can. If we understood everything about her physical make up and her background, we should be able to explain all her actions in terms of circumstances beyond her own control, just as has been done for the two defendants whose cases are apparently special. In fact they are not special at all. Why should *some* kinds of chemical in the brain and *some* kinds of environmental influence count as a defence, but not others? The influences which formed all my clients, and were the direct cause of their crimes, were entirely beyond their control. I contend, therefore, that none of them should be blamed or punished for what they have done.'

It seems, then, that we face a difficult problem. On the one hand it does seem quite unfair to hold people responsible for actions that were caused by influences entirely beyond their control. On the other hand, once we start to allow this kind of excuse there seems no reasonable point at which to stop. Of course we cannot yet provide the physical and environmental explanation of everything everyone does, but we can already explain a good deal and our knowledge is increasing all the time. Perhaps one day we may be able to explain all behaviour in this kind of way. And if so, why should we excuse some people (whose behaviour we have managed to explain) while punishing others (whose behaviour might be explained in just the same way if only we knew enough)? Can we be right to blame people for actions and characters *which have not been explained by science so far*, when an explanation may appear at any time?

What this illustration shows, therefore, is how very easy it is for doubts and qualifications to assail our ordinary ideas about choice and responsibility and blame, and how quickly those doubts, once admitted, threaten to undermine the whole structure of our belief in freedom of the will. *We* are not responsible for what we do; our physical natures and our environments are responsible. *We* do not choose our characters and the actions that result from them; they are chosen for us, by forces entirely beyond our control.

1.2 THE THREAT FROM DETERMINISM

There are many paths to scepticism about freedom of the will: this one, the encroachment of scientific explanation into the area of human choice, is only one of them. It is, however, the most familiar in our culture, and it stems from a serious tension between traditional and scientific ideas about human nature.

Our most familiar ideas about ourselves are rooted in the traditional view that there is a radical difference between ourselves and the world of natural objects and forces that we inhabit. We have of course always thought of ourselves as *partly* natural: our bodies have always been supposed to belong entirely to the natural world, and subject to natural laws. Traditionally, however, we have always thought of ourselves as of dual nature, with one part – the important part – transcending the natural world and quite different from it. It is to this part that our thoughts, desires, decisions and actions have traditionally been attributed; and notwithstanding any doubts that may be creeping in now, we still describe people and their activities in terms quite different from those used to describe what goes on among other things.

To clarify what these differences are, consider another imaginary incident. Suppose that as a result of the combined demands of employers, children, your spouse, the cat and replacement window salesmen you decide that the only possible time on get on with your OU work is in the small hours of the morning; and then, just as you begin to get into a productive routine, some new neighbour (doubtless under the same kind of pressure) takes to practising the trumpet – exceptionally badly – between one and three in the morning. Polite requests and telephone calls to the police have no effect, and you eventually decide that you have no alternative but to take matters into your own hands. Before your neighbour comes home one evening (so that there is no maddening noise to upset the balance of your calm deliberations) you think through various possible courses of action, and eventually recall the plot (somewhat implausible, but never mind) of a detective story you once read. Accordingly you make your way into his practice room, artfully loosen the fittings of the heavy chandelier in the middle, and slightly shift his chair and music stand so that they are directly underneath. At one in the morning the noise starts again as usual, the vibrations finsih your loosening work, there is a crash, and you get on with your essay in peace.

 Exercise

Answer the following questions *quickly*, saying what your immediate, everyday response (before philosophical doubts start to arise) would be.

1   According to the account given, was your decision to fix the chandelier a genuine choice, made of your own free will?

2   Were you responsible for your action, and, at least to some extent, for its outcome?

3   On the assumption that the murder of infuriating neighbours is not morally justified, do you deserve blame and perhaps punishment for your action?

4   As you were deliberating about what to do during the evening (before you reached your decision) was the course of events bound to go the way it did, or *might things have gone otherwise?*

 Discussion

It seems to me that in ordinary circumstances we should say without much hesitation that:

1   The choice as described, was certainly made of your own free will.

2   You were responsible for your action and its outcome.

3   You do deserve blame and perhaps punishment for your action.

4   Things might indeed have gone otherwise. If you had made a different *choice* (to resort to ear plugs, for instance, or to abandon your OU work) or if the musician had *chosen* not to play any more or to sit in a different part of the room, the course of events would have been quite different. As long as people's choices come into the matter, the course of events may go in all kinds of different ways according to what those choices are.

 Exercise

Now consider, in contrast, a small part of the same event, this time not involving any human activity. Think of the time when the musician is in place and the music just starting up, and of the course of events from then on. The vibrations continue the loosening of the screws, and the chandelier falls. How do the ways in which we think about this part of the event differ from the kinds of ways in which we think about the wider event involving people and their choices? Try to think of at least two major ways. Use the four questions in the previous exercise as a guide.

✿ Discussion

The most obvious difference between the incident as a whole and the part not involving people, suggested by the first three questions in the previous exercise, is that the second case contains no conscious agent. Questions relating to choice, responsibility and blame, therefore, simply do not arise. The chandelier does not make a *decision* or perform an *action*: things merely *happen* to it.

But the narrower incident would normally be thought of as different in another extremely important respect as well, suggested by the fourth of the previous questions. Given the situation at the time, the subsequent course of events is regarded as *inevitable*. What happens is bound to happen, as the result of a series of causes and effects determined by the laws of nature. Given the original looseness of the screws, the frequency and amplitude of the sound waves, the force of gravity, the minimal resistance of air and all other such matters, nothing else *could* have happened; and if we had known about all such things in enough detail we could infallibly have predicted the course of events. Matters seem quite different when they involve conscious agents. As long as you were thinking about how to cope with the problem all kinds of future events were possible, and what actually happened depended on the choice you eventually made. But in any system of inanimate objects the course of events is inexorably determined by the natures of the things in the systems – chandeliers, sound waves, gravity and all the rest.

This is one of the main differences between the ways in which we think about ourselves and about the natural world. The natural world has traditionally been thought of as *deterministic*: as working inexorably in a series of causes and effects determined by the laws of nature, so that if we knew all there was to know about those laws and about the arrangments of things at the beginning of time, we could in principle predict the whole course of events ever afterwards. It is this belief that is the basis of science. The aim of science is to understand the workings of nature with a view to explaining, predicting and to some extent controlling the course of events; but if we thought that nature behaved erratically, with chandeliers and sound waves somehow acting according to whim, there would be no point in looking for natural laws.

Our belief that we are different from the rest of nature in not being subject to determinism – in being able to initiate actions that are not determined by the previous course of events – has always been essential to our traditional view of ourselves. It is now a long time, however, since this belief was first seriously challenged. Bentham, for instance, as you have seen (p. 14), believed that determinism applied to people. The basis of his belief in the possibility of a science of human nature was the idea that people's actions could in principle be explained in just the same way as the workings of sound waves and falling objects, and that if we knew enough about how people worked we could predict the choices they would make with total certainty. This was a minority view at the time, but since then there has been an enormous amount of progress in genetics, neuroscience, psychology and many other relevant areas of enquiry. It has become increasingly reasonable to suppose that people can, in principle, be understood in just the same way as the rest of nature, and are as subject to determinism as everything else. And if that is so, is it really reasonable to think of our actions as significantly different from events involving ordinary objects?

If everything about the world – including our part of it – is deterministic, the future is not genuinely open: everything is laid down in advance. We think and deliberate, certainly, and we act on the basis of those deliberations, but our thinking and deliberating are only *part* of the deterministic causal sequence, not interruptions of it. As we wonder what course of action to take we may be under the impression that the future remains unsettled until our decisions are made, but it is in fact already absolutely certain what those decisions will be. No matter how hard we try to change the course of events we can only succeed in continuing it.

And if that is so, how can we possibly justify our traditional belief in what we call freedom of the will? Look again at the first exercise on p. 44, and think about the ways in which we ordinarily describe ourselves and our actions; and then see what happens to these ideas if determinism does apply to us as well as the rest of nature. According to the story you made a choice about what to do, but if it was a predetermined choice, bound from the beginning of time to go the way it did, can it possibly count as free? Can you count yourself as having made a genuine choice when only one outcome of your deliberations was ever possible?

The same problem arises with responsibility. Responsibility is a tricky concept (one of the many that cannot be dealt with at all fully here), but one thing seems certain: we cannot be resposible for anything beyond our power to influence. By no stretch of the imagination, for instance, can we be regarded as responsible for housing problems on the outer planets of Alpha Centauri, or for failing to warn a brontosaurus on this spot a few million years ago that it was about to start eating an indigestible tree. If, therefore, our choices were laid down and bound to go the way they did before even brontosauruses (let alone we) existed, it seems quite out of the question that we should be considered responsible for them. And if we are not responsible for them, we are surely not entitled to praise or blame for them. You are no more to blame for your decision to silence your neighbour than the chandelier would have been if it had fallen, through a series of accidental happenings, without any assistance from you.

And what about our normal belief that whenever we are wondering what to do there are many possibilities about the future course of events, and that the future is open until we make our decision? If determinism is true, that belief seems to be another illusion. We may not know in advance which decision we are going to make, but really it is inevitable long before we make it. It is determined by our physical and mental constitution, which is in turn determined by other events which made us what we are. When we make our choices we think we could have done otherwise, but really we could not.

So if determinism is true, it seems, we are just things like everything else in nature. We are differentiated from inanimate nature by our thoughts and feelings, and from the rest of animate nature by our intellects, but these begin to look like a kind of cosmic joke. They do not make us free. All they do is make us capable of having illusions of freedom, which at least things like chandeliers and even cats are spared.

 Exercise

As revision for this section, answer briefly the following questions.

1   What kinds of belief do we have about ourselves when we claim to have freedom of the will?

2   What is the *problem* of the freedom of the will?

3   What is meant by determinism? (What is the world like if it is deterministic?)

4   Why does it seem that determinism is incompatible with freedom of the will?

 Specimen answers

1   Typical beliefs we have about ourselves, which constitute our belief in freedom of the will, are that when we choose to act in particular ways we could have done otherwise (and therefore could have made the course of events other than it in fact was), that we alone determine which choices we make, that our choices are between genuine options, and that we are responsible for our choices. (Your list may well have differed from this in detail; there is no single correct answer.)

2   The problem of the freedom of the will is of whether we are *justified* in thinking of ourselves in these ways.

3   If the world is deterministic everything that happens is caused inevitably by what went before: the whole course of future events was laid down at the beginning of time.

4   If the world is deterministic, then when we apparently choose what to do only one outcome was ever possible, and we could not have done otherwise than we actually did. This does not seem like free choice. And we cannot be responsible for what we do, because everything we do was laid down in advance by forces beyond our control. (Again, you may well have expressed this differently.)

1.3   THE ALTERNATIVE: INDETERMINISM

The problem we are concerned with is of whether we are justified in thinking of ourselves as we normally do: as responsible for our actions, capable of making other choices than the ones we actually make, and so on. These are the ideas that constitute our belief in freedom of the will. The arguments of the last section seem to have made the first step towards the answer, by showing that *if* we are determined we are not free. Not surprisingly, then, many people who think that we are right to believe in freedom argue that we are not subject to determinism.

Probably the largest group of these consists of people who continue, in spite of the advance of science, to hold traditional ideas about human nature. Perhaps *some*, or even many, of our mental attributes can be physically explained (people who take this view are likely to say), but there are limits: no matter what the physical constraints of our lower natures there is still an element of us that is distinct from these, capable of making totally free choices and allowing us to rise as far above our natural limitations as we choose. Nature may be deterministic, but the scientific explanation of the human mind can only go so far, and the part of us that transcends nature also transcends determinism, and is therefore free.

People who take this line of resistance to determinism have also been joined more recently by another group, who embrace a new source of hope in the claims of modern physicists that even nature is not deterministic at the subatomic level. If this is true, they claim, then even if we do belong entirely to the natural world we are still not subject to determinism, and are therefore free.

So, on various grounds, many people argue that determinism does not apply to us, and that our traditional beliefs about freedom of the will remain justified.

Now the obvious question this raises is of whether they are right in thinking that the world — or at least our part of it — is not deterministic, or whether people like Bentham are right in thinking that it is. It looks as though we need to settle the question of determinism in order to settle the question of the freedom of the will. However, one thing you will find about philosophers is that they are notoriously often unwilling to try to answer obvious questions, and this is not just because they are perverse or simply do not know the answers. Often, for one reason or another, the obvious question is not the most important one to ask; and here, in fact, there is a much more fundamental question that needs to be asked first. (It is, by the way, at this point that the problem of the freedom of the will starts to become complicated and difficult, so do not be surprised if you find the going rather slow.)

People who claim that determinism does not govern us and that we are *therefore* free are in fact taking it for granted that if we can escape determinism, freedom follows as a matter of course. But is this presupposition correct? We have of course already seen an argument — quite a persuasive one — to suggest that if we are determined we are not free. But what about the other way round?

✸ Exercise

If the argument of the previous section is correct (if, in other words, it succeeds in showing that if we are determined we are not free) does it also show that if we are *not* determined, we *are* free? (This question is purely about logic. You may find it helpful to work it out with diagrams or analogies.)

Discussion

The answer is that it does not. The argument so far has apparently shown that

1   if we *are* determined, then *we are not* free
    (determined → not free).

From this it follows that

2   if we *are* free, then we *are not* determined
    (free → not determined)

But it does *not* follow that

3   if we *are not* determined, then we *are* free
    (not determined → free).

The argument which supports (1) also supports (2), but it does not support (3).

If you cannot see that point immediately, it may be helpful to consider an analogy. Analogies often help in the disentangling of philosophical problems (and not just for beginners) because they can make it possible to think about the structure of arguments without having to struggle with difficult ideas like freedom and determinism at the same time. There will be several more in this text.

Imagine, then, that as you are trying to work in the small hours, tormented by your neighbour, you realize that if the music goes on you will never get your essay written (music → no essay). This is the same as realizing that if you are to get your essay written, the music must be stopped (essay → no music). But it does *not* follow that if the music is stopped the essay will necessarily get written (no music → essay), as you can easily see by thinking of all the other things (employers, children, spouses, cats, nervous breakdowns and simple lack of inspiration) that might come between you and the writing of an essay. The technical way of expressing this is to say that although the evidence shows that the music's stopping is *necessary* for the writing of your essay, it does not show that it is *sufficient.*

In other words, the evidence which convinces you that if the music goes on there is no chance of getting your essay written is enough to show that if it is to be written the music must be stopped, but it is not enough to show that if the music is stopped the essay will get written. To show that, you need separate evidence. In the same way, the argument which shows that determinism prevents freedom is enough to show that if there is to be freedom there must not be determinism, but it is not enough to show that if there is no determinism there will be freedom. They show that the falsity of determinism is *necessary* for freedom, but not that it is *sufficient.* If it is also sufficient – if if is enough to guarantee freedom – we need to show that separately.

Our first problem, then, is not to find out whether we are subject to determinism or not. It is rather to find out whether *if* we are not subject to determinism (or, to use the usual term, if our part of the world is *indeterministic*), we shall indeed be free.

In the last section, when we were considering the effect determinism would have on freedom, we started by clarifying exactly what was meant by determinism: by saying what a deterministic world would be like. Presumably, then, we should proceed by doing the same thing for indeterminism.

 Exercise

Think back to the last section and say what a completely deterministic world would be like. Then use your answer to say what an *indeterministic* world would be like.

 Discussion

The world is deterministic if everything that happens is *caused* – brought about

inevitably – by what went before. In a fully deterministic world the whole future course of events is laid down from the beginning of time.

The world is indeterministic, therefore, if at least some things are *not* caused by what went before: if some things happen *without any cause*, and the course of events is not completely laid down from the beginning.

If you answered that question quickly you may perhaps have said that since a deterministic world is one in which everything is caused, an indeterministic world must be one in which *nothing* is caused. But it is not necessary to go as far as that. The world would fail to be deterministic (i.e. one in which everything was caused) as long as anything at all was uncaused; it would not be necessary that everything should be uncaused.

So, if a deterministic world is one in which everything is caused, then an indeterministic world is one in which some things are *not* caused. To deny that the world is deterministic is to say that some things happen without any cause.

Now this is only a clarification: the account of what indeterminism is follows logically from the account of what determinism is. Nevertheless, a great many people who have no difficulty at all in understanding the concept of determinism seem to be completely taken by surprise when they realize what denying determinism actually involves. It literally does mean *accepting that there are such things as uncaused events*: events which are wholly or at least in part *without any cause at all*. And to this they often respond by saying that there cannot possibly be such things as uncaused events: that everything *must* have a cause. In reply to this, various things can be said.

The first and most obvious is that if you think uncaused events are impossible (if, that is, you think indeterminism must be false), it follows that you must think determinism is true, and this may well place you in a position of some perplexity. Many people who think they believe in freedom of the will want to reject determinism because that *seems* incompatible with freedom, but they may now find themselves unwilling to accept indeterminism as well, because they cannot believe that uncaused events are possible. And, of course, if they cannot accept the possibility of uncaused events, that forces them back into determinism, and, apparently, into having to accept after all that we are not free. You may well have found yourself in this uncomfortable position, and if so you will need to decide how to deal with it.

However, although that is the most obvious reply to the claim that uncaused events are impossible, it is not the right one to make in this context. It is important to be clear about what has been going on in this section so far. Nothing that has been said is meant to imply that there *are* such things as uncaused events. The purpose has been only to clarify the *meaning* of the word 'indeterminism': to explain what an indeterministic world *would* be like. You can clarify the meaning of a word (like 'unicorn') without implying that any such thing exists; in fact you need to know what words mean before you can even start to find out whether anything corresponding to them exists. Our purpose at the moment is only to try to discover whether we would be free *if* indeterminism were true, and to work that out we need to be clear about what the concept of indeterminism is. We can do that without having to decide whether indeterminism is true or not, just as we could argue earlier that *if* determinism were true there would be no freedom, without having to decide whether it was actually true or not.

Therefore, even if you are convinced there can be no such thing as an uncaused event, you need have no difficulty in understanding the *meaning* of 'indeterminism' as a state where some things are not determined – not caused by what went before – just as you can understand the meaning of 'unicorn' without believing that unicorns exist. And rather as you might ask questions about what things would be like if unicorns *did* exist (such as whether they would interbreed with ordinary horses) you can also try to establish whether, *if* uncaused events could occur, they would make freedom of the will possible. Let us then concentrate on that question.

Exercise

Suppose the world is indeterministic and that *genuinely uncaused events* keep interrupting the chain of causes. Referring to the arguments about determinism and freedom, try to work out the extent to which indeterminism would help to give us the freedom determinism seems to deprive us of. Do this by imagining uncaused events interrupting the sequence of causes in various places, and consider the results. This is not at all easy, but see how far you can get before you read the extended discussion below.

 Discussion

As a brief guide to why determinism seems to preclude freedom look back to the answer to question 4 at the end of Section 1.2 (p. 47). Can indeterminism help with these problems?

Certainly from the point of view of the first point made in that answer indeterminism seems promising, because if the world is indeterministic the course of events is not laid down from the beginning of time. It is genuinely unpredictable, even in principle. In an indeterministic world our actions, and the events following our actions, might have been otherwise. If you are in a fully deterministic world as you sit wondering what to do about your tiresome neighbour, the result of your deliberations is already a forgone conclusion and has been so from the beginning of time; but if you are in an indeterministic world the future is genuinely open, and anything might happen. So to that extent indeterminism certainly seems an improvement on determinism.

But what about the other elements of freedom that concern us? We do want it to be possible for interruptions to occur in the deterministic chain of causes and effects, certainly, but that is not enough. We want not just *any* interruptions, but interruptions which are *produced by us,* of our own free will, and for which we are therefore *responsible.* Can indeterminism help with that aspect of the problem?

Think again of the sequence of events leading up to your deciding to put a stop to your neighbour's music. If the world is deterministic your decision was caused by your state of mind, which was itself caused by your physical and mental make up and all kinds of external influences, all of which in turn were brought about by a sequence of uninterrupted cases and effects going back to the beginning of time. You were not responsible for all the things that caused the choice, and therefore, it seems, you were not responsible for the choice. But now suppose uncaused events interrupt this sequence at various points. Can they make you responsible for your decision?

Suppose, for instance, that among the events leading to your present state of mind some were entirely uncaused, so that your being in the state of mind which led to the decision was not deterministically brought about. Does that help to make the choice yours, more than it would be in a state of determinism? As far as I can see it makes no difference at all. The problem about determinism was that you could not yourself be responsible for being in the state of mind that led to your choice; but if some of the events that made you what you were, were themselves uncaused, that surely does not help *you* to be responsible for them. In fact an uncaused event is by its very nature one that *nothing whatever* can be responsible for. If determined (caused) events that cause your character to be what it is prevent your being free *because they were beyond your control,* exactly the same seems to be true of undetermined (uncaused) events.

Suppose now that uncaused events occur at other points in the sequence of events. Suppose, for instance, that the choice you make is *itself* uncaused – by your previous state of mind or by anything else. Does that remove the difficulties of determinism, and make it your *free* choice?

This is a question of rather more complexity, and there is much controversy among philosophers about it. But it seems to me, and to very many others, that it really does not help in the least. If an uncaused happening in your mind – for which no one is responsible – is the cause of your *choice*, it is surely even *less* your own *choice* than one deterministically produced by your own character and previous state of mind would be. At least the deterministic one is connected with your character and desires (deterministically produced though these may be); an uncaused event, by definition, comes out of *nothing*. Would you feel that your decision to silence your neighbour was more your own if *nothing* caused it than if your own nature did? If not, it is hard to see how indeterminism can provide the responsibility we normally associate with freedom.

The situation, then, is apparently this (and if you have found that last three paragraphs rather difficult, concentrate on this simple summary). If there is determinism there is no freedom, because if everything that happens was determined from the beginning of time we cannot freely choose, or be responsible for, any of it. But the only difference between a deterministic world and an indeterminisitic one is that some of the determined (caused) events are replaced by undetermined (uncaused) ones for which *no one and nothing* can be responsible. That can hardly make *us* responsible for them.

We seem, in other words, to have landed in very deep waters. We started this section with the idea that if we could prove determinism false we could rescue our belief in free will. We then raised the question of whether indeterminism really would be *sufficient* for freedom – enough to guarantee it. And now we seem to have arrived at the conclusion not merely that it would fail to guarantee it, but that indeterminism is actually as much of an *obstacle* to freedom as determinism is.

So appeals to traditional ideas about human nature or to uncaused events among subatomic particles, even it they are justified, do not help in the least to justify our ideas of freedom of the will. If this argument is right, it is impossible for us to make real choices or be genuinely responsible for anything, whether the world is deterministic or whether it is not. We are caught either way. And since the world must be either one or the other, it seems to follow that freedom of the will is impossible.

 Exercise

As revision for this section, answer briefly the following questions.

1   People who claim that we can show that we are free by showing that we are not determined are making a presupposition. What is it?

2   What does 'indeterminism' mean? (What is the world like if it is not deterministic?)

3   To what extent can indeterminism solve the problems for freedom of the will presented by determinism? Why?

 Specimen answers

1   They are presupposing that if we are not determined, we must be free. If this is true it needs to be proved, because it is not a consequence of the argument that if there is determinism there is no freedom.

2   If the world is indeterministic it is *not* the case that everything is caused by what already exists: some things happen without any cause.

3   Indeterminism is an improvement in the sense that if the course of events is not fixed in advance, the choices we make are not fixed by past events. But one of the problems about determinism was that it seemed to show that we were not responsible for what we did. Indeterminism does not seem to make matters any better, because all it does is substitute uncaused events for some of the caused ones, and uncaused events are by their nature ones for which *no one* can be responsible. In an indeterministic world some events are not caused by past events, but they are not caused by *us* either, and that seems necessary for freedom.

1.4   TWO KINDS OF NON-EXISTENCE

If the problem of the freedom of the will is understood as the problem of whether we are justfied in thinking of ourselves in the various ways we have been considering, these arguments seem to provide the answer: we are not free. This is an exceedingly uncomfortable conclusion for most people, and there are different ways of reacting to it.

One possibility is to go in for straightforward obstinacy: to disregard the argument and refuse to budge from habitual ways of thought. Like Dr Johnson, the eighteenth-century man of letters, who in this context just asserted 'The will is free, and there's an end on't', there are many people who will say such things as 'I don't care what the argument says; I believe God has given us freedom', or 'I know I'm free, and I'm not going to be put off by any argument that seems to prove I'm not'.

It is obviously pointless to try to argue with people who take this kind of line. Since they have declared that they intend to take no notice of the arguments presented already, they obviously intend to stick to their views no matter what any argument may show. If people are not interested in trying to understand these important issues and are unwilling to question their beliefs there is not much you can do about it, except treat them as having retired from the discussion. Holding to beliefs irrespective of what reasons may be given against them is just not an intellectually serious option. Some people, it is true, do try to make a principle of following intuition rather than reason, but although that sounds quite good as rhetoric it does not stand up to even the most cursory scrutiny. For instance, not many people are impressed when their *opponents* stick to their own intuitions and resist all argument and evidence against them. Most people who claim that intuition is more reliable than reason are in fact happy to use reason as long as it leads to conclusions they want, but resort to claims about the importance of intuition whenever reason seems to be leading them into difficulties.

If just rejecting the argument is not an acceptable option for anyone who is concerned to reach the truth about these matters, does it mean that anyone who takes the argument seriously must accept the conclusion and all that follows about changing our attitudes to ourselves? Does it mean that we must stop thinking we can influence the future, or make genuine choices, or be responsible for our actions and their consequences?

Perhaps that may indeed turn out to be necessary. The unwelcomeness of the conclusion is not enough to show that it must be wrong. This kind of thing is an occupational hazard of philosophy: you can no more do philosophy without risk to habitual ways of thought than you can do science without risk to established beliefs. If the arguments are conclusive, and our ideas of freedom are simply unfounded, we may just have to start thinking differently.

On the other hand, we can certainly be cautious about leaping to hasty conclusions. No one who is intellectually serious can just take a Johnsonian attitude to unwelcome conclusions; but before we revise our ways of thinking quite as radically as the arguments seem to suggest, we can at least put some effort into seeing whether anything has gone wrong with them. When a conclusion is so much at odds with what we normally think, it is perfectly legitimate to work on the basis of the *hypothesis* that something may have gone wrong somewhere in the argument, and to try to work out what. This is quite different from Johnsonian denial.

Our original problem was to find out whether we were free or not. Now that a negative answer has been given to that question, therefore, the problem for anyone unwilling to accept it is to try to find something wrong with the argument that led to it. To do that we need to enquire more closely into the conclusion reached so far, which is interesting for more reasons than just being startling.

The original question we asked about freedom of the will was simply *whether it existed* or not. (The question of whether we have freedom of the will is the same as the question of whether freedom of the will exists in creatures like us.) So far we seem to have reached the answer not merely that it *does* not exist, but that it *could not possibly* exist, under any circumstances whatever. The distinction between what *does* not exist and what *could* not exist is an important one which considerably affects the approach to the problem of the freedom of the will, and it needs to be explained.

Questions about whether things exist are very familiar. For instance, we may wonder whether the Loch Ness Monster exists, or whether there is (exists) intelligent life elsewhere in the universe, or whether there is (exists) an Open University student over the age of a hundred and ten. When we ask these questions we are considering different possibilities about what the world is like: it may be one way, it may be the other (intelligent life elsewhere or no intelligent life elsewhere). We understand the alternatives – we know (more or less) what the world *would* be like in each case – and we are interested in which way it actually *is*.

The question of the freedom of the will is usually presumed to be a question of this sort. We think there are two possibilities: the world may be such that we have free will or it may be such that we have not, and the question is which.

However, the argument that freedom was incompatible not only with determinism but also with indeterminism completely alters that way of looking at the matter. *Whatever* the world is like it must be either deterministic or indeterministic, and therefore, according to these arguments, whatever it is like it cannot contain creatures with freedom of the will. That is quite unlike the case of intelligent life elsewhere in the universe, because even if that could somehow be proved not to exist we still know that if the history of the universe had been different it might have existed. The conclusion of the argument about freedom, on the other hand, is not only that freedom *does* not exist, but that it *could* not have existed *even if the world had been different*.

Why is it that some non-existent things would have existed if the world had been different, while others are so thoroughly non-existent that they could not have existed even if it had been different? Once again, it may be easiest to explain by way of analogy.

Consider, then, a matter much more familiar and less complicated than problems about freedom and determinism. Imagine that we are running a computer dating agency whose aim is to match everyone with perfect partners. Our claim is that if such partners exist we will produce them, and we are at present about to try to meet the requirements of two new female clients who are hopeful that we shall be able to find their dream men.

We interview the women in turn, asking each about her likes and dislikes, noting her complaints about men who have not been to her satisfaction, and generally prodding and probing until we feel we have a good idea of what she wants. By the end of the session with the first, we see that her ideal man turns out to be intelligent, brave, generous, handsome, kind, chivalrous, faithful, recognising the equality of the sexes, sensitive to the fair division of labour, and so on. She is not claiming *ever* to have seen such a man, of course; that is why she has come. She has, prompted by our questions, just put together a list of qualities she likes, and has given that bundle of ideas the label 'dream man'; and now she wants us to feed it into the computer and find someone corresponding to it. We do this, but the result is negative, and we are not surprised. We were sure that no such paragon had found his way on to our list; and, furthermore (let us say for the sake of the story, since this illustration is of course purely fictitious), we are in serious doubt that any creature of the kind exists at all.

 Exercise

If we believe that such a man almost certainly does not exist, and want to convince our client, what kinds of argument might we produce? (Do not go to great lengths to make the answer here true of even plausible. All that matters is the *kind* of argument that would be relevant.)

Discussion

We might start simply by claiming that we had looked at enormous numbers of men but never found one like that. Then we might quote historical sources and sociological or anthropological studies, which conspicuously failed to record any such men. Or we might go deeper still into the evidence of evolution, and claim that since human males were designed by nature to be set on nothing but producing as many offspring as possible by as many women as possible, they were bound to be competitive, selfish, bullying, inherently unfaithful, and quite unconcerned about the interests of women. Or, at a different level, we might talk about the effects of male hormones on the personality, and argue that wherever there was testosterone there was bound to be trouble.

In general, then, if we want to argue that the hunt for this ideal man is bound to fail, the way to proceed is to call on evidence about *the way the world is*, and claim that *because of the way it is* men corresponding to our client's ideal almost certainly do not exist in it.

Now we move on to the second woman, who turns out to present more radical problems. When we refer to our notes at the end of our interview with her we find that what would please her is a slender, beefy, fair, dark, dreamy, practical character who is rugged and independent while following her with a dog-like devotion and being attentive to her every wish. This time we are absolutely sure we cannot come up with anything to suit her.

 Exercise

If we want to convince this woman that her ideal does not exist, what kind of argument should we use?

 Discussion

Here the case is quite different. It is certainly true that our computer would find nothing corresponding to the description, that historical records would show that no such man ever existed, and that no evolutionary or genetic evidence would support the conclusion that he could possibly exist. But on the other hand we know in advance that it is not even worth looking at the evidence. This ideal man *certainly* does not exist; but in this case the reason has nothing to do with the workings of evolution or unsatisfactory side effects of male hormones. There can be nothing corresponding to this description *because the description itself is incoherent.* What it says in one place is contradicted in the next. It is as though the woman had said that her ideal house would be a spherical cube, or her ideal pet a two-horned unicorn.

In this case, therefore, we can know that no such man exists without doing any investigation of history or anthropology or genetics at all: *whatever* the truth about evolution or hormones, nothing could possibly exist corresponding to the description. Meeting our client's specifications in one respect actually involves going against them in another. No matter what we produced, therefore, she would always complain that we had not given her what she wanted.

The general point is this. When we ask whether something exists we have in mind an idea (concept, description) and what we want to know is *whether the world contains anything corresponding to that idea.* So, for instance, if you ask whether unicorns exist you are asking whether the world contains anything corresponding to the description 'white horse with a single horn', and the answer is (presumably) that it does not.

But now think of the way any description works. Think of the description of a unicorn, for example: white, horse, single horn. If we are to understand anything by the word 'white', we must understand not only when it is appropriate to use it, but also, by implication, when it is not. The word 'white', if it is to mean anything, must *exclude* various possibilities, such as being red with black spots. Again, the meaning of 'horse' excludes all sorts of things, like having feathers. You do not know what a horse is unless you know that the jackdaw nesting in your chimney is not a horse.

If you say that a unicorn is white (all over), therefore, you are saying by implication that it is *not* a great many other things, such as black with red spots; and in that case anything that is black with red spots will fail to meet your specifications of what a unicorn is. Conversely, if you say that a unicorn must be black with red spots (all over), anything white will fail to meet your specifications. So, if you say that to count as a unicorn an animal must be white *and* black with red spots (all over, at the same time) you make it impossible for *anything* to comply with your specifications, because anything that met one part of the description would necessarily fail to meet the other part.

What all this shows is that there are two quite different ways in which any woman's ideal man might fail to exist; or, to put it another way, two quite different reasons why the world might fail to contain anything corresponding to her description. On the one hand, men might simply fail to rise to the heights of her specifications. On the other hand, the specifications she was putting forward might themselves be incoherent.

Now (at last) let us return to the subject we are supposed to be discussing, and consider the point of this extended analogy.

Its principal moral is that when an enquiry is being conducted into whether or not something (such as an ideal man) exists, or whether something (such as any of us) has a particular characteristic (such as freedom of the will), that enquiry should really be thought of as taking place in two stages. In both cases the question is about *whether something corresponds to a particular concept*, and in theory the first thing to do is check that the concept is of a kind to which anything *could possibly* correspond. If it is not, there is no point in starting to investigate the world to find out whether anything actually does correspond to it. The second enquiry has point only if the concept itself turns out to be coherent.

In practice, we usually leave the first step out because there is no problem about it. In the case of the first woman, we took it for granted that we had a clear idea of what she meant by her dream man, and we moved straight from compiling her list of requirements to feeding it into the computer and seeing whether we had anyone corresponding to it. And at the outset of this enquiry it seemed as though the problem of the freedom of the will was of just the same sort as this. In other words, we missed out the first of these two steps, and took it for granted that we had a clear idea of what we *meant* by freedom of the will, and the only question was of whether we had it (corresponded to the idea) or not.

Then, however, the argument took an unexpected turn. It appeared that freedom was incompatible with indeterminism as well as with determinism, and therefore that it could not exist *no matter what* the world was like. And that makes the case look much more like that of the second woman, whose ideal man could not exist no matter what was true about evolution and such matters, because the various elements of her idea were actually in conflict with each other.

Does this mean, then, that our earlier conclusion that we did not have free will resulted from a self-contradictory concept of freedom, to which nothing could possibly correspond? It certainly looks possible, so we should look back again at the idea of freedom we have been working with, and try to see if there is any such problem about it.

This is not at all easy to do; the argument is quite complicated (and it should be said in advance that you will not be asked for its details in any exam or TMA.) However, it is worth trying to explain it.

Once again the analogy may help. When we were interviewing clients, according to the account given, we did not merely ask them what they wanted: we also made more general probings and listened to their complaints about men they had encountered. That was how we pieced together the second woman's incoherent ideal. It was quite an important element in the story that we should have to *work out* a description of her ideal from the various things she said, because it is most unlikely that any client would actually *state* that she wanted someone fair and dark in the same breath: the contradiction would be too obvious. When people have inconsistent ideas they are usually not obviously inconsistent, or they would not be held.

In the same way, we are not likely to go around with ideas about freedom which are obviously incoherent. If they are so, we shall have to excavate to find the incoherence; and again we can probably best do this indirectly. It we look at *why both determinism and indeterminism seemed to rule out freedom* (the equivalent of noting the characteristics which would prevent someone from counting as a particular woman's ideal man) we should be able to work out by implication what would count as giving us freedom.

What was it, then, first about determinism and then about indeterminism, that made them both seem incompatible with freedom? Think back to the chandelier episode again.

It is obvious that you did in one sense make a choice when you decided to loosen screws and move music stands: your going into the room with the necessary equipment and starting work was the result of your desires and intentions, and not (for instance) something you did while sleepwalking. Your desires and intentions were (roughly speaking) the main cause of the happening. Why then did it seem that in a completely deterministic system this apparent choice would not be a *real* choice, for which you were genuinely responsible? It was that the state of mind which caused the action was itself brought about by the previous state of the world: it was fixed in advance, before you even existed. It seemed, therefore, that the choice could not count as *freely* made by you, or as something you could be responsible for, since no other outcome was possible. Other things than you were ultimately responsible for all aspects of what happened.

Why, on the other hand, did this state of affairs seem not to be improved by indeterminism? Because even though what you did was not laid down from the beginning of time, you were *still* not responsible for the state of mind which brought the action about, because nothing can be responsible for an uncaused event. So, according to this account, what gets between us and freedom in both cases is our not being responsible *for the states of mind that cause our actions*. And if that makes us *not* free, it follows that in order to *be* free we should have to be *responsible for those states of mind*.

Now of course people will argue that you can be responsible for your own state of mind. If you drink too much you are responsible for being in a frightful temper the next day; or (it is said) if you go in for yoga or deep breathing or various other things you can be responsible for putting yourself in a calm state of mind. You can alter your state of mind by taking drugs. This is of course true, but then the question arises of where the states of mind came from that made you choose to take the drugs or do the deep breathing, and even if you claim that those states of mind resulted from previous choices, it is obvious that this process can only go back so far. What is quite certain is that you cannot have chosen to be in the state of mind that resulted in *the first choice you ever made*. You cannot be the *ultimate* cause of the state of mind you are in, because to do that you would have had to be responsible for your own existence and nature. That means *you would have had to exist before you existed*.

If we are complaining that we cannot be free unless we are ultimately responsible for being *the kind of person making the choices*, therefore, the complaint is a very remarkable one. It is as though our second woman had been demanding a man so considerate that he always consulted her about everything, and then complained, when he tried to consult her, that he had not consulted her about consulting her. It is not quite the same confusion as complaining about men who are fair and men who are dark at the same time, but it is confused in that no state of affairs that could be described would give her what she wanted: no matter what was produced her specifications would still not be met. It seems to me that the idea of freedom that demands *ultimate* self-determination is confused in exactly the same way. We know what we mean by wanting to make choices, but we get into (infinitely) deep waters if we complain that we are not free *unless we also choose to be in the state of mind from which each choice arises.*

It appears, then, that the reason why the earlier arguments showed that freedom was impossible (i.e. incompatible with both determinism *and* indeterminism) was indeed essentially the same as the reason why the second kind of ideal man was impossible: it was that the concept of freedom we were working with was one to which no state of affairs could possibly correspond. It is (as it were) not the fault of the world that it does not contain freedom of the kind we want; it is our fault for wanting something self-contradictory, so that *whatever* the world was like we should still be dissatisfied.

 Exercises

As revision for this section, answer briefly the following questions.

1   Explain the kind of question we are asking when we want to know whether things of a certain kind exist.

2   What are the two stages involved in enquiries of these kinds?

3   Why (in very general terms) are there no:

> Dodos
> Carnivorous herbivores
> Martians
> Married bachelors?

4   Referring to your answers to questions 2 and 3, say why (according to the arguments presented here) freedom of the will seems not to exist.

 Specimen answers

1   We are asking whether the world contains anything *corresponding to a particular description* (concept, idea).

2   The first stage is to make sure the concept in question is coherent, so that something *could* correspond to it. Only then should we go on to the question of whether anything or some particular thing does in fact correspond to it.

3   Dodos and Martians do not exist just because of the way the world happens to be. Dodos once did exist, but were made extinct by the depredations of another species; Martians do not exist partly (at least) because the atmosphere and temperature of Mars cannot support complicated life forms. If the universe had been different both might have existed. Carnivorous vegetarians, however, do not exist because 'carnivorous' *means* 'meat eating' and 'vegetarian' *means* 'not meat eating', so anything that met one specification would *ipso facto* fail to meet the other. The same applies to married bachelors, since 'bachelor' *means* 'unmarried man'.

4   According to the arguments given here, freedom of the will turned out not to exist because it failed at the first of the hurdles mentioned in question 2. The concept was one that nothing *could* correspond to. The failure of freedom of the will to exist was like the failure of carnivorous vegetarians and married bachelors, rather than that of dodos and people on other planets.

1.5   THE PROBLEM REVISED

Let us once again review the position we have reached. We started this enquiry with what seemed a fairly straightforward question: the question of whether or not we had freedom of the will. At first it seemed as though the answer would depend on whether the world was deterministic or not. We could not be free if the world was deterministic, so the problem for anyone who wanted to prove that we were free was to show that the world was not deterministic. But then it was argued that indeterminism was as unhelpful for freedom as determinism was, so that whatever the world was like we could not be free. And then in the last section I argued that the source of this remarkable conclusion was in fact an incoherent concept of freedom, to which nothing could possibly correspond.

This is probably a rather surprising thing to discover – at least I found it so when I first encountered the idea – and it is a kind of surprise that is always lying in wait for philosophers. You follow familiar ideas in directions you never tried before, and frequently find yourself led to conclusions of a quite unexpected kind. It is like going down a path of a very familiar garden, and suddenly spotting a turning you have never noticed before. It may come to a dead end, or it may reveal wonderful new vistas, or it may wind insidiously into a quagmire. Philosophy is much concerned with exploring unfamiliar byways of our systems of ideas; and very often, as we explore, we encounter totally unanticipated problems.

It is probably not surprising that there should be such scope for exploration and discovery in our ideas, once you think about it. Our systems of thought and language are extremely complex, developing in all kinds of different circumstances, stretched and adapted to fit all kinds of needs, and containing far too many ramifications and complexities for us to have any hope of grasping the whole structure at once. It is rather as though thousands of people in thousands of different places were working on parts of a huge building, moving around and joining the work in different places to some extent, adding little bits here and making adaptations there, but generally working without any overall plan and concentrating on each local part at a time. It would be inevitable that as the building progressed, and as people got a wider view of it, there would be surprises. Some of these would simply be interesting and pleasant: short cuts where only circuitous routes had been known before, or charming courtyards produced quite by accident. But there would also be problems about different parts that simply did not fit. Walls, as they progressed towards each other, might turn out to be out of alignment; huge towers might turn out to have been built on foundations laid by someone else with another purpose in mind, and quite inadequate for the present structure; windows which had once overlooked open spaces might now confront blank brickwork.

Philosophy is rather like this. New discoveries are made all the time about hidden complexities in our system of thought. Sometimes they are purely interesting and illuminating, but very often we find confusions: parts which do not match other parts, and systems of belief which turn out to have hardly any foundation at all. We then have to try to decide what to do about these problems.

In the case that we have been studying here, what started out as a straightforward problem about whether something existed or not has now turned into a quite different kind of problem. There is no point in asking whether we have freedom of the will (whether we correspond to the idea of a being with freedom of the will) if that idea itself is confused. The first problem for anyone who wants to prove that freedom of the will does exist is to find a coherent *concept* of freedom. Only then will there be any point in trying to show that something actually does correspond to it.

But what *exactly* is our new problem? What is involved in finding a coherent idea *of freedom*? What is the criterion for deciding whether we have successfully found one?

Think again of the problem we face in trying to find the second woman's ideal man. Her ideal appears to be incoherent, and we know there is no point in looking for anything corresponding to the current specification. We know, therefore, that the first thing we need to do is find a coherent description of a suitable man. But how can we possibly do this? Suppose, for instance, we try to help her by finding a coherent specification as close as possible to her incoherent original. She cannot have both fair and dark at once, but perhaps her complaints about the dark seem a bit less bitter than her complaints about the fair, so we settle for dark; she cannot have both independent and clinging, so we settle for clinging . . . and eventually we put together a nice, coherent description. But she is most ungrateful. This is nothing like her ideal man, she complains: he isn't fair, he isn't independent. We cannot solve her problem, she says, by producing a coherent description of something *other* than her ideal.

Now of course we can reply that her own description is no use as a basis for solving her problem either, since nothing could possibly correspond to it. But that does not necessarily mean that we have to conclude that her problem is insoluble. What we can do is go back again to where she started, with the *effect* she wants her ideal man to have. She wants someone who will please her in all respects. Now in trying to decide what that was, we made the quite reasonable assumption that we should pay attention to her statement of her likes and dislikes, her criticisms of men who had not met her expectations, and so on. We certainly found that by that method we ended up with an incoherent description. Maybe, however, there was something wrong with our initial assumption, given that our real concern was to identify a man who would please her in all respects. Perhaps we should not have taken her own immediate reactions as definitive, but looked more deeply into her psychology. It *might* just be possible to identify a totally satisfactory man in some quite unforeseen way; perhaps, for instance, we might realize that if she were satisfied in some particularly fundamental respect, other things would suddenly cease to matter.

In the case of freedom of the will the position is rather similar. We need a coherent description of a state of affairs we should be willing to count as freedom before we look to see whether we are in that state; but on the other hand if it is to count as part of a solution to *the problem of the freedom of the will* there are specifications that the description will have to meet. To satisfy people who are anxious about the freedom of the will it will need to have the *consequences* people want, in allowing them to keep intact their beliefs about autonomy, choosing between genuine alternatives, responsibility, desert and all the rest. So far it looks as though this is impossible. Perhaps, however, we have made a wrong assumption somewhere. Perhaps if we looked hard enough we might be able to find a wrong turning somewhere in the argument, and discover after all there was some way to put together a coherent account of freedom of the will that would satisfy us. Then we could go on to the second part of the question, of whether we did actually correspond to that idea.

That is the nature of the present problem. Can we find a coherent way of describing a state of affairs that would give us all the things we normally associate with freedom of the will? Or must we settle for something less?

 Exercise

As revision for this section, briefly explain the difference between the problem of the freedom of the will as it appeared at the beginning of this text, and (according to the argument given here) as it appears now.

 Specimen answer

We originally took it for granted that we knew what we *meant* by a being with free will, and that the problem was simply to find out whether we corresponded to the description or not. It now seems that our concept was incoherent, so before we can answer the first question we need a concept that is coherent *and* includes everything we normally associate with freedom of the will.

1.6 ONE POSSIBLE SOLUTION

Philosophers have for centuries been trying to defend our usual beliefs about freedom of the will against arguments like the ones developed here, and since people tend to be extremely ingenious in defence of beliefs that are essential to their ideas about themselves, there are a great many different ways in which the defence is attempted. Obviously we cannot go far into all this ingenuity here. There is, however, one kind of approach that is so important and influential that some discussion of it must be included.

It is an approach that leads to what are known as *compatibilist* solutions to the problem of the freedom of the will, for reasons that will be explained in the next section. The method of reaching this kind of solution depends on *clarifying the central concepts at issue* in problems about freedom of the will: concepts such as choice, responsibility, having the power to do otherwise, and so on. The claim of philosophers who adopt this line of argument is that the problem of free will arises only because of misunderstandings and confusion about such ideas. If we do as we obviously should, they say, and make sure we have a proper understanding of the questions before we start to answer them, the problem simply disappears.

The arguments that follow this general line vary considerably in detail and sophistication. Here, for the sake of illustration, we shall keep to the simplest version.

Start, then, by considering again what is worrying people who are concerned about freedom of the will. Think of the kinds of questions they ask. We apparently make choices, but *could we really have done otherwise than we did*? Are we really *responsible* for what we do? And so on: you are already familiar with the kind of question.

Now although in trying to answer these questions we have found ourselves in considerable philosophical difficulty, it is striking that the questions themselves do not seem at all obscure. The words in terms of which they are expressed – 'free choice', 'responsibility' and all the rest – are not the property of philosophers. We all use them regularly without a second thought and without any problems at all. And we are, after all, the arbiters of what our words mean: they mean nothing more than we, the speakers of the language, mean by them. In order to understand the questions properly, therefore, what we should do is clarify the ordinary meanings of the words and expressions involved.

This is a matter of understanding how the words and expressions are *used*. If you were a foreigner coming here and trying to learn the meanings of these words, you would have succeeded when you were able to produce them in the circumstances the natives agreed were correct, and not otherwise. To understand what it meant to say that something was black, for instance, you would have to know that it would be appropriate (true) to say 'that is black' if you were pointing at a heap of coal, or the print on this page, or my shoes, but inappropriate (false) if you were pointing to a trumpet, or a picture of a unicorn, or Arthur Marwick's cravat. Until you know the circumstances under which 'this is black' would be true and false, you do not understand what it means.

This is the principle we should apply in trying to understand the various freedom-connected ideas we are concerned with. So for the sake of clarifying the matter let us imagine a small band of foreign investigators, without much knowledge of English, briefed by their local anthropological institute to work out the natives' (i.e. our) concepts of freedom of the will and related matters. Their problem is to go through the list of terms that crop up in discussions of freedom of the will, and try to work out their meanings by establishing the principles according to which native English speakers do and do not use them.

Let us also suppose that they conveniently arrive just in time to catch an epidemic of desperate OU students all over the country plotting in various ways to put a stop to the nocturnal music of inconsiderate neighbours. You with your chandelier are just the beginning. Everywhere students and their friends and relations are sneaking into the offenders' houses and flats, pouring noxious substances into whisky bottles on sideboards, sliding swamp adders down bell ropes, sawing through strategic floor boards and (less drastically) pouring glue into pianos and trumpets. Some act alone, some conspire with fellow students, others bully hapless spouses or force other students at gun point to do the dirty work for them. Some act while sleepwalking. Some formulate elaborate plots, but are prevented from carrying them out by prudent friends who lock them in or drug them, or by falling branches which stun them before they can reach their object. All in all there is plenty of variety, and the anthropologists make careful notes of all the incidents and of the terms in which the natives describe the aspects of them connected with freedom and choice. Then, on the basis of their observations, they try to work out the meanings of the various words and expressions involved.

In fact the freedom-related terms are so very pervasive in our language, and the complexities of their use so considerable, that the full report of their research will fill a massive tome. Fortunately, however, a brief outline of a selection of the findings will be perfectly adequate for our purposes, as will appear.

What follows, by the way, is expressed for reasons of space in the form of a straightforward narrative, but it could easily have been done in the form of exercises and discussions. After the first illustration you may like to see how you yourself would analyse each of the expressions discussed before seeing what is said about it in the text.

The researchers start with what seem to be the simplest concepts, trying to establish the meaning of *choice* and other related words ('doing deliberately', 'deciding' and so on). Under which circumstances do the natives agree that it is and is not appropriate to use such terms? They all agree that you *chose* (decided) to go and loosen the chandelier, and that others *chose* (decided) to put foreign substances into the musician's whisky, or *deliberately* put snakes down bell ropes. When do they think such words are not appropriate? Well, the musician who drank the whisky was found dead on the floor, but no one believes that the student in question had any intention of *killing* him; she thought she had only put a sleeping drug in the bottle. The neighbours say that although she *chose* to put the substance in the bottle, she didn't choose to put *that* substance in, or to kill him; those were accidents. They also say that the man who was knocked out by the falling branch didn't choose to spend the evening lying on the ground; that was an accident too.

So, after a little thought, the linguistic team summarizes its findings (very briefly and roughly – their full report is of course much more careful and detailed) by saying that the natives' criterion for using the word 'choice' is that the direct cause of the happening in question is the agent's own desires and intentions. What English speakers mean by saying that you *chose* to loosen the chandelier was that your desires and intentions were the direct cause of your loosening it. Conversely, when what happened was in spite of, or irrespective of, an agent's desires and intentions, there was no choice.

The next term they find on their check list of key concepts is the idea of *free* choice; or doing things *of one's own free will.* Here they have a bit more difficulty, because for a long time it seems as though these mean nothing more than simply choosing. Every time the researchers find a case of choosing they ask the natives whether they would count this as a case of free choice, or of something done of the agent's own free will; and the reply always seems to be that they would. You chose to loosen the chandelier, and, indeed, it was a free choice: you did it of your own free will. The man who put the adder down the rope did what he did of his own free will, as did the woman who sawed through the floorboard. Eventually, however, the researchers do come across a few cases where the natives agree that although there was choice of a kind, it was not really *free* choice. They mention, for instance, the woman who put glue in the piano only when her husband threatened to commit suicide if she did not find a way of putting a stop to the noise. She made a choice of a kind – she could have decided to stay at home and risk the suicide – but it was not really a free choice. There is also the student forced into activity by another holding a gun at his head. Again, he made a choice of a kind – he chose to act rather than be shot – but it was not at all free.

In the light of examples like these the researchers conclude (in their brief summary, even less accurate than the previous one) that choices are not counted as free when they are made because of some kind of special constraint. Otherwise, all choices are free choices.

Next they investigate a matter of particular interest: the meaning of expressions like 'you could have done otherwise'. These are very important, because when we start to doubt that we have freedom we wonder whether we could ever have made choices other than the ones we actually did make.

What do these expressions mean? The researchers do not find it difficult to establish a general pattern. The natives seem to agree that you could have done otherwise when you fixed the chandelier: you could (as suggested earlier) have resorted to earplugs or given up the OU course. The man with the snake and the woman with the poison could also have done otherwise, as indeed could even the woman with the suicidal husband and the man with the gun at his head. The ones they agree could not have done otherwise are ones like the sleepwalker, and the students prevented from the fulfilment of their designs by prudent friends and providential accidents.

The brief conclusion reached in the light of these observations is that 'you could have done otherwise' means roughly the same as 'what you did was the result of your choice'. Conversely, you could not have done otherwise if you had no choice – because, for instance, you were locked up or knocked out.

Then, finally, they tackle the problem of responsibility. This is probably the most complex issue of all, partly because the issue of responsibility is usually inextricably entwined with questions of morality. However, even though there is often a great deal of disagreement among the natives about whether it is appropriate to say that someone is responsible for something or not, making it very difficult for the researchers to establish what the meaning of the expression really is, some things are clear. For instance, people are always responsible for making the choices they do rather than others that are available to them. You are responsible for deciding to go and fix the chandelier; the woman who put the substance in the whisky bottle is responsible for doing that; and even the man with a gun at his head was responsible for choosing to go along with the demands of the gunman rather than staying put and risking being shot. In fact, whenever anyone has a choice, they are responsible for making the choice they do rather than the others available.

Responsibility for the *consequences* of a choice is a trickier matter, because the eventual outcomes of your decisions are likely to be influenced by all kinds of matters which are entirely beyond your control. Most people agree that you are responsible for the damage you caused to your musician (though some say he was responsible for bringing it on himself); but they are more divided about what to say about the woman who poisoned her musician when she only intended to drug him (though if someone else had changed the packets without her knowing they would probably say that person was responsible for the musician's death); and most of them say that the gunman, rather than the student being coerced by the gunman, was really responsible for the death. The people who were clearly not responsible for anything were the ones who were locked in, unconscious, hypnotized, or miles away from what was going on.

The complexity of all this is such that the research report on the meaning of 'responsibility', and the analysis of the findings, will on its own take up a very large proportion of the final report. However, the very brief summary is that responsibility seems to be a matter of how much depends on an agent's *choice*. To the extent that agents could have made things different by making different choices, they are responsible for what happens; if what happens has little or no connection with their choices, they are not much or not at all responsible. Responsibility is a matter of the extent to which what happens depends on actions which are brought about by the desires and intentions of people.

I said before that these extremely brief and inaccurate summaries of the meanings of a small sample of freedom-related expressions would provide enough information for our purposes here. What has been said, although very scanty, is enough to make clear a general pattern of meanings of these expressions, and (as you will see if you experiment) it applies equally to all freedom-related expressions. If you think about it, you will see that all these words and expressions are used to convey *the extent to which what happens depends on the desires and intentions of people*. What is *chosen* is what is caused by those desires and intentions; what is *freely chosen* is what is chosen in the absence of particular kinds of outside interference; *you could have done otherwise* whenever your choice was what determined what happened; and so on. Some things that happen are strongly connected with our choices, others not at all, and many more to a greater or lesser degree. The freedom-related expressions all indicate degrees of connection between events and choices.

These, then, are the findings of the imaginary anthropologists about the meanings we, as the users of the language, give to freedom-related expressions. Now think again of the point of what has been going on in this section.

What we needed was a clear and unconfused *concept* of the freedom of the will before we could go on to ask the question of whether we did in fact meet the required specifications. Our belief in freedom of the will amounts to the belief that we can make free choices, that when we choose to do one thing we could have done another, that we are responsible for what we do, and so on. Now we know what it *means* to be in these situations we can go on to ask whether we are actually free.

 Exercise

Now, *given the definitions just established*, try to answer the questions we started out with.

1   When we make choices, are they really free choices (made of our own free will)?

2   When we make a choice is it really possible that we could have done otherwise than we actually did?

3   Are we responsible for the choices we make?

Then, given that these things constitute what we mean by freedom of the will, say what the consequences are for the question of whether or not we have freedom of the will.

 Discussion

Given the definitions, the answers to the questions are:

1   Sometimes, when there is serious interference, our choices are not made freely. Most of our choices, however, *are* free, so of course we *can* make free choices.

2   Whenever we make a choice we could have done otherwise, because what it means to say that we could have done otherwise is that what we did depended on our choice.

3   We are always responsible for making the choices we make rather than the others available to us, and we are often responsible for the outcome of those choices (depending, roughly, on the extent of which the outcome was in our control).

The problem of the freedom of the will, at least as defined in this text, is of whether we are justified in thinking of ourselves in the way we normally do – as capable of making free choices, being able to do otherwise than we actually decide to do, and being responsible for our actions. Since it is clear that we often do make free choices, that we could always have done otherwise when we make choices, and that we are obviously always responsible for our choices, we are obviously justified in thinking of ourselves in these ways. We therefore have freedom of the will.

According to this line of argument, therefore, the problem of the freedom of the will is solved, and this time positively. We have not only found a coherent account of what is meant by having freedom of the will; once we have that account we can immediately see that we are indeed free. It is as though, having found a coherent description of a man who would completely satisfy the second woman, we realized to our surprise that he had been living round the corner all the time.

 Exercise

As revision for this exercise, briefly answer the following questions.

1   Give some examples of freedom-related words and expressions.

2   What is the point of trying to clarify the meanings of freedom-related expressions?

3   What, in general, does the function of all freedom-related expressions turn out to be?

4   How (according to the arguments given here) does clarifying these expressions provide a solution to the problem of the freedom of the will?

 Discussion

1   Expressions referred to in the text have been 'choice', 'decision', 'free choice', 'doing of one's own free will', 'the possibility that one might have done otherwise', 'responsibility', and so on. You could, however, add indefinitely many others: 'real choice', 'genuine options', 'having the power to make different choices', 'having the power to change the course of events', 'being able to determine the course of your own life', and so on. In fact you could add any of the expressions you would normally use in describing people and their activities but would not use in the description of events among inanimate objects (or even possibly other animals – though that raises many complications).

2   Our problem is to find the answers to various questions about ourselves, and in order to answer those questions it is necessary to be clear about the meanings of all the words and expressions involved.

3   They all distinguish between what is dependent on our choices (comes about as a result of our desires and intentions) and what is not.

4   The problem of the freedom of the will was of whether we were justified in thinking of ourselves in particular ways. When the meanings of the terms involved are clarified, it immediately becomes clear that we are indeed justified in doing so.

1.7   COMPATIBILISM AND ITS CRITICS

You may or may not be persuaded by this proposed solution to the problem of the freedom of the will, and the question of its adequacy will be returned to shortly. Before this is done, however, it is important to say a bit more about this kind of approach to the problem, since one of its most important aspects has not yet been mentioned. You may have noticed already that according to this line of argument the question of whether we have freedom of the will has been answered, positively, *without raising any questions about determinism*. According to this kind of analysis determinism makes no difference to the question of freedom: freedom and determinism are *compatible*.

 Exercise

Before going on, see whether you can explain why this is.

 Discussion

Think again of what this analysis has shown about our use of freedom-related words and expressions, and the general pattern that has emerged. It turns out that we use these expressions in general to distinguish between situations where (roughly) what happens is *caused by us in accordance with our desires*, and situations where what happens is *caused in other ways*. In saying, for instance, that you could have done otherwise when you went on your chandelier-fixing expedition, whereas the fellow student who was locked in by his friend and the other who was knocked out by a branch could not have done otherwise, you are saying that what you did depended on your desires and intentions but what happened to them did not depend on theirs. The expressions distinguish, in other words, between *different kinds of cause*. However, they are still both *kinds of cause*. Since determinism is simply a state where everything is caused, freedom and the rest as defined in this section are quite compatible with determinism.

If you find this puzzling, think again about why determinism originally seemed incompatible with freedom of the will. The problem seemed to lie in the origins of the desires and intentions which are the cause of our actions. If the desires and intentions which led to your going into your neighbour's house were the inevitable product of causes set in motion before you were born, it seemed that your choice of action could not be free, and that you could not be responsible for what you did. But, says the compatibilist, this idea rests on a quite mistaken understanding of the meaning of expressions like 'free choice' and 'responsibility'. If you look at what they really mean – the ways we, as language-users, actually use them – you will find that they have nothing to do with the *origins* of desires and intentions at all. They all take those desires and intentions as given, and then distinguish events that are caused by them (i.e. chosen) from events that are caused by other things.

 Exercise

Try working this out with a specific incident – perhaps the woman who decided to put drugs in the whisky. Explain why, according to the original arguments in Section 1.2, determinism seemed to prevent her choice from being a real choice, and then say why the compatibilist would argue that this conclusion was mistaken.

 Discussion

Her decision to put drugs in the whisky was caused by her state of mind and environmental influences at the time, but if the world is deterministic both those things were brought about by chains of causes laid down since the beginning of time. There was only one possible outcome of her deliberations – things were bound to go the way they did – and if only one outcome is possible there cannot be a real choice. But, says the compatibilist, this is not the right way to think about things. If you ask what we *mean* when we say the woman had a real choice, you will see we mean that what happened *depended on what she decided*: that *if* she had decided not to act, or to put glue in the piano instead, that is what would have happened. The meaning of the expression 'real choice', if you think about it, turns out not to have anything at all to do with where the choice came from, but only about the extent to which what happened depended on what choice was actually made.

According to this kind of theory, then, freedom can exist *within* determinism. Freedom and determinism are after all compatible, which is why theories of this kind are called compatibilist. Their supporters claim that the problem of the freedom of the will arises only because a mistaken understanding of the various concepts involved leads to the mistaken conclusion that determinism would rule out freedom, and that once that mistake is put right the problem disappears.

So is this right? Does the compatibilist succeed in solving the problem of the freedom of the will?

There are certainly many philosophers who think so; compatibilism of one form or another (there are many variations of detail) is probably the most widely accepted kind of solution to problems of the freedom of the will. Some philosophers, indeed, talk of *dissolving* rather than solving the problem, since they claim that it disappears as soon as it is properly understood, though that way of putting things is not as common now as it was twenty or thirty years ago. Most versions of the theory are supported by more sophisticated arguments than the appeal to ordinary language outlined in the last section, but all of them depend on the idea that once you clarify the concepts involved, and as a result understand the question properly, the question is easy to answer: of course we are free in any understandable sense. Our worries that we might not be, and our anxieties about determinism, stem only from confusion.

To other people, however, this so-called solution to the problem of the freedom of the will may seem nothing but a miserable sleight of hand: the sort of trick that gives philosophers the reputation of playing with words. Compatibilists may have provided a meaning – even the most usual meaning – for expressions such as 'real choice', 'responsibility' and so on, and may have shown that according to these definitions we certainly can make real choices; but (the dissatisfied are likely to say) the meanings they have given to not correspond with what *we* meant. Compatibilists have given these terms *different* meanings from the ones we had in mind, and then shown that according to these other meanings freedom does exist. That is rather like proving that unicorns exist by redefining 'unicorn' as 'creature with at least one horn' and then showing that there are plenty of them around. It may be easy to prove that freedom of the will exists according to *that* definition; but as that *is not what we meant* they have not proved that what *we want* exists, and therefore have not shown that we are justified in thinking of ourselves in the way we normally do.

Who, then, is right; compatibilists or their critics? We can start by noting in passing one small but quite important part of the overall problem that the compatibilist account of the matter does seem to sort out. At the very least, it shows that we are justified in going on using all the freedom-related words. They have a clear and useful function. That is no small matter, since many people who find themselves lured into scepticism about freedom of the will react by feeling that all terms connected with choice, freedom, responsibility and the rest should be expunged from the language. But does compatibilism really solve the whole problem? Does it show that we are justified in thinking of ourselves in the way we usually do, and that we really have all the attributes we think of when we say we believe we have freedom?

Given that way of expressing the problem of the freedom of the will, I suppose that to some extent the answer must be a personal one. The question concerns what we normally think and want to think about ourselves, and this may well vary between people. Perhaps some may believe and desire nothing more than the compatibilist offers. There is no doubt, however, that a great many people will want more, for the simple reason that what they want is not in the least compatible with determinism.

According to the compatibilist account we are free *even if* everything about the course of our lives was fixed long before we or even our planet existed. Most people, when they say they want freedom, would regard no such state of affairs as giving them freedom. Most of us take it to be part of freedom that the future should be genuinely unfixed – genuinely open – waiting for our decisions about what to do before what will eventually happen is set in motion. The same is true of responsibility. There may be some sense in which we are responsible for what happens if we cause whatever it is by our intentions; but if those intentions are ultimately beyond our control then we are not responsible *in the way we want.* What we want is *ultimate* responsibility, not a thin kind of responsibility which is dependent on our being ultimately lucky or unlucky to have the kind of character we have. Unless we can actually interrupt the deterministic course of events, change the course of things, and be ultimately responsible for doing so, many of us will say we have not got what we mean by freedom of the will.

In other words, it well seem to many people that the compatibilist definitions of freedom-related terms, according to which we have freedom of the will, are much too *weak*. They leave too much out. What such people want is freedom according to much *stronger* definitions of these terms: defintions which carry implications of the possibility of interrupting the otherwise deterministic course of events in ways for which we are fully and ultimately responsible.

If the weak definitions seem satisfactory to you, compatibilism may well solve the problem of free will to your satisfaction. If they do not it will seem to you, as it seems to me and to many other philosophers, that the compatibilist account of freedom does not solve the problem. Such philosophers are, unsurprisingly, known as *incompatibilists.*

Nevertheless, even if the compatibilist account of freedom does leave out elements essential to your own ideas, there is still a claim the compatibilist may be able to make; and this is essentially the line taken by the more sophisticated kind of compatibilist. The reason why many people think the problem of free will has not been solved is that the compatibilist account of all the freedom-related terms is too weak: we want more than these definitions include. But anyone who thinks the compatibilist account is inadequate still needs to show that *any other coherent account of their meaning is possible.* We are back to the original problem of finding a coherent account of what it is to be able to initiate changes in the otherwise deterministic course of events, and to have ultimate responsibility, without getting into the incoherence of wanting to be the cause of our own existence. The compatibilist may, therefore, be able to claim that even though these meanings of the words *are* weak, in leaving out all sorts of elements that matter to us, they are nevertheless the strongest that can be had. The strong concepts we want just *cannot* be made coherent.

My own view, at least at present, is that this conclusion is probably right. This is of course a controversial opinion: many philosophers, called *libertarians,* do think (or at least hope) that they can, in spite of all these arguments, show that our ideas about freedom can be made to fit coherently together, and that we really are free in the fullest possible sense. But there are probably very many more who think that this cannot be done, and that even though compatibilism may not give all we want, it probably provides as much as is possible. What we really want – ultimate self-determination – is actually incoherent; and in that case we may have to settle for the compatibilist account, not as a positive solution to the problem of the freedom of the will (one which would show we were free in the way we had always thought), but as the only account of freedom, choice, responsibility and all the rest that makes sense.

If so, we are in the postion of the woman who must eventually resign herself to recognizing that the concept of her ideal man really is incoherent, and that there is no possible description of someone who will meet all her requirements. The man round the corner, inadequate as he may be, probably does represent the best that can even be imagined. What she must do now, therefore, is start revising her plans to take account of there being nothing better than this disappointing creature. What we must do, similarly, is see what the implications are of having to settle for a much weaker kind of freedom, compatible with determinism, than we had originally hoped.

Exercise

1 Explain the meanings of 'compatibilist', 'incompatibilist' and 'libertarian'.

2 What shortcomings do some people think a compatibilist account of freedom has?

3 Give one merit of compatibilism which survives even if you accept these criticisms.

4 What (in the text) is meant by *weak* and *strong* meanings of freedom-related words and expressions?

Specimen answers

1 A compatibilist thinks that freedom of the will and determinism are compatible, an incompatibilist thinks they are not. A libertarian thinks that it is possible to find

a coherent account of freedom which has all the consequences we normally associate with freedom, and that we are free.

2   Although a compatibilist account does give coherent meanings for all freedom-related terms, they are not the meanings many people have in mind because they leave out too much. They do not adequately represent what such people believe when they claim they have freedom of the will, because the kind of freedom they are thinking of is not compatible with determinism.

3   The compatibilist account shows that it is reasonable to go on using all freedom-related terms in spite of scepticism about freedom of the will; they make distinctions which are important in ordinary life.

4   The weak meanings are the ones given by the compatibilist, according to which the terms do nothing more than specify the degree of connection between what happens and the desires and intentions of people. They are described as weak because they leave out a good many of the ideas people have in mind when they use these various terms, and which are included in the *strong* meanings: ideas like having the power to initiate changes in the deterministic course of events and having ultimate responsibility for actions. According to the arguments presented here, the weak meanings may be the only coherent ones.

2 THE CONSEQUENCES

2.1   PUNISHMENT AND ITS JUSTIFICATIONS

Because our ideas of freedom of the will are so closely bound up with the way we think about ourselves, the consequences of having to modify these ideas are likely to be very far reaching. There is, for instance, the question of the way we should think about the course of our own lives, and our projects and hopes for the future, if the best we can have in the way of freedom is compatible with determinism. There are also problems about our reactions to other people, and what to think about such things as anger, indignation, gratitude and the like if people cannot ultimately help being the way they are. Here, however, I shall concentrate on the problem which is most familiar in the context of discussions of freedom of the will: our ideas of praise and blame, desert, and reward and punishment. The issue is a very striking and important one, and it is one where the philosophical arguments seem to have far-reaching and serious practical implications.

If the foregoing arguments are right, they show that we are responsible for our actions in the *weak* (compatibilist) sense that they, and often their outcomes, are caused by our choices (our desires and intentions), but not in the strong sense of being *ultimately* responsible for them. Ultimately, according to these arguments, we are lucky or unlucky to be the kinds of people we are, in the circumstances we are in, and making the choices we make. But if this is so, what becomes of our familiar assumption that if people choose to do wrong they deserve blame and punishment, and that if they act virtuously they deserve praise and reward? It is easy to argue that this is quite unjustified.

Suppose, for instance, I am a thoroughly vicious character: suppose I go around mugging little old gentlemen and being cruel to animals and cheating in exams and scattering litter around. I may have to agree that you would be justified in keeping me away from other people so that I could not do harm; but I shall argue that it would be quite unfair to *blame* me for my actions, let alone *punish* me.

Punishment is a matter of doing unpleasant things to offenders in response to the unpleasant things they have done. Although I choose to do all these unpleasant things, and I am therefore to that extent responsible for them, I still did not choose to be what I am. It is my *misfortune* to have this vicious character, and therefore, ultimately, my misfortune that I choose to act in these unacceptable ways. How, then, can it be right for you to add to my misfortune by heaping extra unpleasantness on to me? It is quite wrong to punish people for what they cannot help. The same applies to praise and reward for virtue. You may have been lucky enough to be born absolutely charming and as a result act virtuously all the time; but how can it be right to reward what is ultimately your good fortune, by adding to your natural advantages?

 Exercise

If you accept the earlier arguments about freedom of the will, must you also accept this argument and its conclusion? Explain you answer.

 Discussion

Your answer may well be something like this.

'It has been shown', you may have said, 'that it would be unfair to punish you just for the sake of doing something unpleasant to you; I quite agree that your ultimate misfortune in being a deplorable character should not be increased by the deliberate imposition of other unpleasantnesses. Nevertheless, there are *other kinds of reason* for inflicting punishment, and the obvious one is that unless we did it, we should have no way of keeping public order. Punishment is justified as long as its purpose is to alter the range of options open to people, so that if they want to choose one of the bad options open to them (like mugging) they realize that it comes in a package, with a stiff sentence attached. When they see that there is such a package they will be deterred from making choices they otherwise might have made; other options will seem more attractive by comparison. And we have to carry through these penalties when they are incurred, because otherwise the whole system would fall into disrepute and fail.'

You may not have expressed the matter quite like that, of course, but it is quite likely that in one way or another, you have argued that punishment can be justified because it is a *deterrent*. If so, what you have done is challenge one element of the foregoing argument, but not the other. You have accepted that it is ultimately people's good or bad luck that they have one kind of character rather than another, and that therefore they do not ultimately *deserve* punishment. Punishment should not be inflicted on them on grounds of desert. Nevertheless, even though they should not be punished on *those* grounds, they may justifiably be punished on *other* grounds. Punishment is justified because it acts as a deterrent to crime, and is therefore for the general good. The deterrence argument is quite different in kind from the desert argument, and may be acceptable even though the desert argument is not.

 Exercise

This kind of argument in defence of punishment may seem familiar to you. Where have you encountered it before?

 Discussion

You have probably spotted that this justification of punishment is precisely the one offered by Bentham. He thought (see p. 12 above) that the only morally justifiable purpose of punishment was to adjust the ways in which it was in people's interests to act. He believed, as you have seen, that most people acted in self-interested ways, and that left to themselves they would act in ways which reduced the total level of happiness in society. If, however, they knew they would be punished for activities which worked against the general good, they would choose to do other things instead, and the total sum of happiness would thereby be increased.

Theories of punishment are of course as complicated and difficult to summarize adequately as other theories dealt with by philosophers, but it is useful to divide them into two broad categories: *retributivist* theories, which essentially hold that a wrong action should be met by a kind of penalty appropriate to the action and deserved by the offender, and *utilitarian* theories, which hold that punishment is justified only in terms of any good consequences that will result from it.

Bentham was led to reject retributivist ideas of punishment by the fundamental moral principles of utilitarianism, according to which all suffering is intrinsically bad, and should therefore never be inflicted unless it will prevent greater suffering. It should not be inflicted *just because someone has done something wrong*, because that, considered on its own, only increases the total amount of suffering. If by inflicting it, however, you can prevent greater suffering (either by preventing the offender from doing further harm or by deterring others from doing the same thing) it is not only justified but morally necessary. Bentham was led to his view of punishment, in other words, by the general principles of his moral theory.

What has been presented in this analysis of freedom of the will is in fact a different argument to the same conclusion. Retributivism holds that punishment should be given in response to its being *deserved*, but, according to the arguments presented here, nothing is ultimately deserved. Even if retributivism were acceptable in principle, therefore, there would never be anything to which it could apply in practice. Punishment on grounds of retribution is therefore always unjustified.

It is not at all surprising that the two subjects being discussed in this introduction to philosophy – ethics and the freedom of the will – should both have consequences for punishment. The question of punishment is a question about how people should be treated, and the answers given are bound to be influenced both by general views about what makes actions right and wrong and by views about what people are like (what the nature of human freedom is). What is particularly interesting is that the two main theories we have been considering – utilitarianism as a theory of ethics and the theory of freedom presented here – both lead independently to the conclusion that retributivist attitudes to punishment are unjustified.

 Exercise

As revision for this section, answer briefly the following questions.

1   What is the difference between retributivist and utilitarian theories of punishment?

2   Why do Bentham and other utilitarians reject retributivist punishment?

3   Why do the conclusions about freedom of the will reached earlier lead to the rejection of retributivist ideas of punishment?

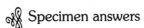 Specimen answers

1   Retributivist theories hold that the purpose of punishment is to inflict on offenders whatever they deserve; utilitarian theories hold that its purpose is to prevent people from acting in ways that will result in greater harm than the punishment causes.

2   Utilitarians reject retributive punishment because, considered in itself, it increases the overall amount of suffering.

3   Retributivist theories hold that offenders should be punished simply because they deserve punishment, but according to this view of freedom of the will no one *ultimately* deserves anything.

2.2   THE PRACTICAL CONSEQUENCES

I said in the introduction to Part II of these units that the problem of free will was like the problems of ethics in being a philosophical issue with serious implications for practical matters. If the foregoing arguments are right it seems that retributivist attitudes to punishment ought to be abandoned. What we need to consider now are the implications of this conclusion in practice, and how far reaching its consequences are.

Start, then, by considering the extent to which current attitudes to punishment are retributivist.

 Exercise

Consider the following statements about punishment, and try to judge whether the speaker holds a retributivist or utilitarian view of punishment. (Be prepared for the possibility that the speaker may be confused.)

(a) Terrorists who endanger the lives of others deserve to lose their own. If we are lenient and shrink from hanging them it will just encourage others to do the same thing.

(b) We ought to be sorry for people from deprived backgrounds. It's not fair to punish them when they commit crimes; they can't help the fact that they were born into a family which couldn't give them any privileges, and the only way they can possibly find any pleasure or success in life is by breaking the rules. It's quite different when someone from a privileged background breaks the law; such people are just greedy and irresponsible, and ought to be punished severely.

(c) It's no good being lenient with drunken drivers. They knew they were going to drive when they started to drink so they've no excuse at all, and they cause thousands of deaths every year. Unless you punish them the killing will just go on. If your child had been killed you would think they deserved very severe punishment.

 Discussion

(a) This speaker seems to be trying to hold both kinds of view at once. The argument about deterring others is utilitarian, but the argument about desert is retributivist.

(b) This argument is entirely retributivist. It is claiming that some offenders do not *deserve* punishment as much as others, by implication because their crimes come more from their circumstances than from inherent wickedness. There is no consideration of the *consequences* of punishment.

(c) This speaker seems confused. The reference to thousands of deaths and stopping the killing seems essentially utilitarian; the idea of the recommended punishment is to cut the death rate. But the reference to the absence of excuse and to what you would think the culprits deserved if your child had been killed are more in line with retributivist ideas.

Arguments like these are very familiar (the first, indeed, was taken directly from a speech by an extremely well-known politician), and if you bear in mind this discussion as you read and listen to people's views about punishment you will go on finding that retributivist attitudes are very widespread. Some people (at least some of the time) have attitudes that are almost purely retributivist; very many more have stong retributivist elements mixed in with otherwise utilitarian views. You will be very unusual if you find no element of retributivism in your own attitudes.

So retributivist views are very widespread; but how much difference would it make in practice if they were replaced by utilitarian principles of some kind? The reason why it is important to be clear about the principles which *justify* punishment is that those principles will also determine who should be punished for what, and in what way, and how severely. The importance of deciding whether to follow retributivist or utilitarian theories lies in their very different implications for the nature of penal policy. Sometimes retributivist and utilitarian theories may lead to the same conclusion about a particular punishment, but since the theories are radically different in kind they will often lead to different ones; and whichever theory you hold should, obviously, determine your policy.

Exercise

Consider the following cases, and explain the extent to which the different theories of punishment would lead to different conclusions about what policy ought to be followed.

(a) The question of capital punishment for murder.

(b) The pursuit of Nazi war criminals who have been for a very long time leading ordinary lives under assumed identities.

(c) The punishment of attempted murder.

 Discussion

(a) Retributivists would simply want the punishment to be appropriate to the crime, and would be likely (though by no means certain) to argue that people who had taken other people's lives should usually forfeit their own. They would probably want to know a great deal about the circumstances surrounding particular crimes, since they would not regard all murders as equally wicked, and might want less severe sentences for some murderers than for others. In general, however, they would always look at *the criminal and the nature of the crime* in order to determine what was deserved by way of punishment.

Utilitarians, on the other hand, would think it inherently bad that even a murderer should suffer, since this, taken on its own, would add to the amount of suffering in the world. They would not want punishment at all *unless* the suffering visited on the criminal would prevent greater suffering, probably by means of deterring future crimes of the same kind. That means that utilitarians would look at the likely *consequences* of punishment rather than the criminal's degree of guilt, and the punishment approved would depend entirely on what the facts about likely consequences seemed to be. They would want evidence about the *least* severe penalty which would have the effect of deterring others from murder, and would probably therefore want capital punishment only if less severe methods were unlikely to have the necessary effect.

How much the two differed in practice would therefore depend on the utilitarian's judgement of the facts of the matter, but they could in principle differ very considerably.

(b) The important thing about these cases is that the criminals in question are not generally known to be criminals, and it is not generally known until the hunt is successful that the perpetrators of the crime still exist. There may also be no reason to think that any of them are going to do any more harm.

To retributivists these facts would be irrelevant. They would presumably regard it as appropriate that the criminals should be punished for their misdeeds even though if they got away with them nobody would know. Once again, however, things are more difficult for utilitarians because their opinion must depend on the likely effects of pursuit and punishment. On the face of it, they would have to say that since the exposure would cause suffering to the victims, while no one would suffer if they were not exposed, it would be better to leave them in peace. (It seems most unlikely that punishment of this sort would act as a deterrent to people in future Nazi Germanies.) On the other hand, there might be benefit to the survivors; it would probably be a considerable consolation to them to see their oppressors punished. Or there might be some less well-defined benefit to the world in general. However, the main difference is that a genuine utilitarian would need good evidence that such beneficial effects would outweigh the suffering of the criminals if they were punished; if there were inadequate evidence a utilitarian would have to resist pursuit and punishment.

(c) Since the intentions and motives of the person are identical in the case of attempted murder and murder, and only incompetence or accident prevents the outcomes from being the same, the retributivist would have to approve the same punishment in both cases.

For the utilitarian, however, this is not the case. A utilitarian is reluctant to punish at all and will approve punishment only if more good will result from it than the punishment itself does harm. But a moment's thought shows that *attempted murder* is not a crime anyone needs to be deterred from, because it is not one anyone sets out to commit. What people set out to commit is *actual* murder. If you intend to fail you are not trying to murder at all; and if people see failed murders going unpunished that will not encourage them to commit successful murders. So while there is every reason to punish murder, there may be no justification for punishing attempted murder: all that should obviously be punished is what the would-be murderer has actually succeeded in achieving, such as assault, conspiracy, possession of dangerous weapons, or whatever.

There is also a more positive argument against punishment, which is that if you have attempted murder and failed, and the penalty for the murder is the same as for the attempt, you have nothing to lose by going on and making another attempt. If you incur as severe a penalty for the attempt as you would for the murder, you might just as well go on and finish the job.

Once again, of course, since utilitarianism has to judge penal policies by their likely consequences rather than by formulating principles of appropriate punishment, there might well be particular circumstances where these considerations were overridden by others. In some contexts there might be evidence that it would deter murder to punish attempted murder, and in that case its punishment would be justified. But even so there would be no *necessary* connection between the punishment of murder and attempted murder. Certainly the utilitarian could not argue that because the evil intent was equal, so should be the punishment.

So, the extent to which the two differ in practice will depend on the utilitarian's judgement of what the consequences of punishment would be in each case. Sometimes the two kinds of theory might coincide in what they recommended; often, however, they would not. And this is, incidentally, why it is not acceptable to say (as many people do) that the purpose of punishment should be both to do what the criminal deserves *and* to deter. Since the theories do not always have the same results you need to decide which to follow in cases of conflict, and if you then allow in considerations based on the other theory you are doing what is unjust by your own standards. If you are a retributivist, for instance, you have a view about the punishment deserved for a particular crime; but if you then increase that punishment to make it more of a deterrent you do what is unjust to the criminal by your own retributivist standards. Confusion about which justification of punishment is being used leads to actions which are unjustified by *either* standard.

A change to thoroughgoing utilitarian theories of punishment would, then, be quite likely to involve considerable change of attiudes and policy. But how difficult would it be to make such changes? How easy would it be for people to abandon the retributivist elements in their attitudes to punishment?

This will certainly differ a great deal from one person to another. Many will find the utilitarian conclusions outlined above very difficult to accept: they will think it intrinsically wrong that murderers might not forfeit their own lives, or that attempted murder might go unpunished when the guilt involved was the same as if it had succeeded. Many others may well think, on the basis of these discussions, that the switch to utilitarian attitudes to punishment might be manageable after all.

However, the discussion so far has emphasized only one aspect of the difference between the two theories of punishment. To see the other aspect consider a more detailed set of cases.

 Exercise

Consider the following cases, and for each:

1 Say what your immediate inclination is.

2   Decide whether it is utilitarian or retributivist.

3   If it is retributivist say what a utilitarian's attitude would be, or vice versa, and compare the two.

In doing this exercise, *discuss the cases as they are given here.* Both utilitarians and retributivists assess what punishment is appropriate according to the facts of the matter, and if you consider a different case you will obviously get a different result.

(a) The government, getting very anxious about the spread of football hooliganism, has changed the law to allow a maximum sentence of twenty years in prison for any crime associated with football matches, and you are a judge about to pass sentence on a young man who was among a good-humoured group of supporters caught breaking windows, apparently just for fun. The defence argues that the crime was a very mild one and the man in question was no threat to public safety; a warning and a fine covering the cost of windows would meet the case. The prosecution argues that it is essential to deter people from getting involved in *any* kind of lawless activity at football matches, and the most effective way to stamp out hooliganism is to use the maximum sentence in all cases, including this one. You accept the facts put forward on both sides. Which way do you decide?

(b) You are living in a racially tense area, where there have recently been riots in which hundreds of people have been killed and injured. A policeman belonging to the dominant race is on trial for the murder of a member of the minority race during the previous disturbances, and everyone in the minority group believes he is guilty, and is howling for revenge. You have very good reason to think that if he is acquitted there will be another riot, with many more injuries and deaths. All the evidence so far is against him. On the other hand, you are about to be called as a witness, and you know he is not guilty; you saw a member of the minority group commit the murder. The outcome of the trial will depend on your testimony. What should it be?

(c) You are a member of the government in a country where there is a serious drug problem, working on possible reforms of the law to make it more effective against the pushers. At present the police make frequent arrests, and if they were able to get convictions most of the pushers would now be in prison and the trouble would have lessened. However, the standards of proof required for conviction are so high that most of the pushers are having to be acquitted. You have good evidence to show that if the required standards of proof were dropped a little you would be able to convict most of the guilty people and stop the menace, but you also have good reason to think that if this happened some innocent ones would be convicted as well. What do you recommend?

Discussion

(a) If you go for leniency you are judging according to desert (the crime was not very serious so the punishment deserved is rather little) and are a retributivist; if you go for severity you are judging according to desirable consequences and are a utilitarian. The utilitarian in this context gives a *more severe* sentence than the retributivist, and so gives *more than* (according to retributivist principles) *the individual deserves.* Although the defendant did nothing very serious he is being given a heavy sentence for reasons of public policy.

(b) Most people would immediately respond to this by saying that it would be absolutely appalling for an innocent person to be punished, and that it is a fundamental standard of justice that this should never happen. If you think this, you will have decided that you should tell the truth, and make sure the policeman is acquitted. If so, however, you will have taken a retributivist line. You will be saying that the policeman does not *deserve* punishment, and that is why you must tell the truth. A utilitarian, however, would argue quite differently. As the case is presented here, a utilitarian would have to lie and convict the policeman, because that would bring about the greatest public good.

(c) You may well have said, as people often do, that it is better for a hundred guilty people to go free than for a single innocent one to be punished, and that the standards of proof should remain very high. Needless to say, however, this is not a utilitarian position, and it does take for granted the importance of desert. From a utilitarian point of view suffering in the innocent is no worse than suffering in the guilty, and if you can do more good by punishing occasional innocent people (or indeed any number of innocent people) than by acquitting them, that is what you should do.

What these cases show, in other words, is that changing from a retributivist to a utilitarian theory of punishment does not just mean refraining from pursuing harmless old men who committed crimes forty years ago, and hanging murderers when no good will come of it. Utilitarians do think punishment *intrinsically* undesirable, because it causes suffering, and do think severe punishment *intrinsically* more undesirable than lenient punishment, and to that extent are generally more inclined to leniency than retributivists; but on the other hand since their overall judgement of what is right in any situation must turn on the facts, there may equally well be occasions when their recommendations for punishment will be more than a retributivist would find just; and, even worse, they will often have to recommend punishment where a retributivist would say there should be none at all.

This is where the greatest problems arise with a utilitarian theory of punishment. Many people's retributivist inclinations will allow then to look with little censure on lesser punishment than is deserved. Far more people think it far worse that punishments should be greater than is deserved, and quite beyond the moral pale that punishment should be visited on the innocent. This is perhaps the most notorious of the many problems confronting utilitarianism.

 Exercise

How are utilitarians and retributivists likely to disagree in *practice* about the punishment of offenders?

 Specimen answer

Since utilitarians oppose punishment except when it will have a positively good outcome, they will often want to refrain from punishment at all (as perhaps in the case of unknown war criminals) when retributivists think punishment is appropriate, or punish less severely than retributivists think is deserved. On the other hand, the reverse can also be true. Because they are concerned with consequences, utilitarians will sometimes want punishments more severe than retributivists think are deserved, and, more serious still, may want to punish or risk punishing the innocent.

2.3 CONCLUSION

In Section 1.7 it was argued that there was probably no way of putting together a coherent account of the kind of freedom most of us thought we had, and that if so we should need to revise rad' ally our ideas about ourselves. If you found that conclusion difficult to accept you will probably find it even harder now the extent of its consequences begin to appear.

However, as I argued earlier, just resisting the conclusions is not an intellectually serious option. If there are confusions and contradictions among our most firmly held ideas some of them must be false, and this must matter to anyone who cares about truth. And just as it is not intellectually serious to pronounce 'the will is free, and there's an end on't', disregarding all the problems of free will, it is not *morally* serious just to assert that it must be wrong to punish the innocent, and think that ends the matter.

Consider, for instance, the position of people who feel strongly about the justice of retributivist attitudes to punishment (probably most of us most of the time). Why do we feel strongly about punishment? At root, presumably, because we think certain kinds of activity, such as causing suffering and death, are *bad*, and that it *matters* when people engage in them. If it is morally important that these things should not be done, it *seems* to follow that they should always be avoided unless there is some overpowering reason for permitting or encouraging them. But retributivists *are* willing to cause avoidable harm: it is about this that they are in disagreement with utilitarians. Retributivists refuse to make the punishment more severe than is appropriate to the crime *even if* doing so would deter future crime and reduce the total of suffering. They also often insist on punishing criminals − so causing suffering − *even if* this will prevent no further suffering. So unless we ourselves are guilty of doing some of the very things we want to punish criminals for doing, we need a very good justification for adopting a retributivist theory of punishment. Unless there is such a justification retributivism causes unjustified harm, and that should be a matter of great concern to anyone who professes moral outrage at utilitarian conclusions.

However, as I also argued before, it is always intellectually and morally serious to *question* any arguments which lead to totally unacceptable conclusions. I suggested in the introduction that if you thought, as the non-stop train went on its course, that the arguments were going wrong you should regard that as a reason for getting off; but another reason why philosophers often insist on stopping is not specifically because they have seen something go wrong with the argument, but because they are so appalled with the destination they have reached that they want to investigate whether anything *may* have gone wrong, and explore different tracks. Before they throw out beliefs which seem to have been proved unfounded, they will go to great lengths to see whether they can after all be justified.

So while some moral philosophers do feel compelled to accept arguments of the kind given here, along with all the uncomfortable consequences that seem to follow from utilitarian attitudes to punishment, others (probably most) believe there are ways of finding coherent moral theories which do less violence to our intuitions. Some, as was mentioned earlier, believe that it is possible to solve the problem of free will in a fully satisfactory way (libertarian or compatibilist), and that there is therefore no problem, from the point of view of free will, about retributivist attitudes to punishment. Others think that it is possible to escape the difficulties by way of quite different theories of punishment, neither retributivist nor consequentialist, which they think avoid the difficulties of both. Yet others think it may be possible to develop more sophisticated forms of utilitarianism, according to which our intuitions about such matters as not punishing the innocent turn out to be justified after all.

My own inclination, at least at present, is towards the last of these, and if our time had not run out we could now return to the problems begun in Part I, and look again at utilitarianism with these new considerations in mind. As it is, however, the remaining questions must be left with you.

You may well have the feeling that the problems have considerably increased, rather than lessened, since you started out. If so you are in good company. Many philosophers are still perplexed by these matters, and find themselves changing their minds whenever they think about them. Nevertheless, however distant the prospect of a satisfactory solution may be, for anyone who cares about the truth of these matters there seems no alternative but to go on looking.

FURTHER READING

General anthologies

Watson, G. (ed.) (1982) *Free Will*, Oxford Readings in Philosophy, Oxford University Press.
Dworkin, G. (ed.) (1970) *Determinism, Free Will, and Moral Responsibility*, Prentice-Hall.
Berofsky, B. (ed.) (1966) *Free Will and Determinism*, Harper and Row.
Honderich, T. (ed.) (1973) *Essays on Freedom of Action*, Routledge & Kegan Paul.

The idea that determinism is irrelevant

Matson, W. (1956) 'On the Irrelevance of Free Will to Responsibility', *Mind*, LXV.
Ayer, A.J. 'Freedom and Necessity', in Ayer (1954) *Philosophical Essays*, Macmillan, and in Watson.
Smart, J.J.C. (1961) 'Free Will, Praise, and Blame' *Mind*, LXX.

Compatibilist views

Hobart, R.E. (1934) 'Free Will as Involving Determinism and Inconceivable Without It', *Mind*, XLIII, and in Berofsky.
Nowell-Smith, P.H. (1948) 'Free Will and Moral Responsibility', *Mind*, LVII.
Nowell-Smith, P.H. (1954) *Ethics*, Penguin Books, chapters 19 and 20.
Dennett, D.C. 'Mechanism and Responsibility', in Watson and in Honderich.
Dennett, D.C. (1978) *Brainstorms*, Harvester Press, chapter 15.
Dennett, D.C. (1985) *Elbow Room*, Oxford University Press.
Glover, J. (1970) *Responsibility*, Routledge & Kegan Paul.

Libertarian views

Campbell, C.A. (1951) 'Is "Freewill" a Pseudo-Problem?' *Mind*, LVIII, and in Berofsky.
Chisholm, R.M. 'Human Freedom and the Self', in Watson.
Wolf, S. (1980) 'Asymmetrical Freedom', *Journal of Philosophy*, LXXVII.
Wiggins, D. 'Towards a Reasonable Libertarianism', in Honderich (this is a *difficult* paper).

Other incompatibilist views

Broad, C.D. 'Determinism, Indeterminism, and Libertarianism', in Berofsky.
Hospers, J. 'What Means This Freedom?', in Berofsky.

Fatalism

Ayer, A.J. 'Fatalism', in Ayer (1963) *The Concept of a Person*, Macmillan.

General

Lewis, H.D. 'Moral Freedom in Recent Ethics', section IV, and 'Guilt and Freedom', both in Sellars, W. and Hospers, J. (eds.) (1952) *Readings in Ethical Theory*, Appleton-Century-Crofts.
Strawson, P.F. 'Freedom and Resentment', in Strawson (1974) *Freedom and Resentment and Other Essays*, Methuen, and in Watson.
Bennett, J. 'Accountability', in van Straaten, Z. (ed.) (1980) *Philosophical Subjects*, Oxford University Press; a discussion of Strawson's 'Freedom and Resentment'.
Nagel, T. 'Moral Luck', in Nagel (1979) *Mortal Questions*, Oxford University Press, and in Watson.

Punishment

Hart, H.L.A. (1959) 'Prolegomenon to the Principles of Punishment', in *Proceedings of the Aristotelian Society*, LX, and in Hart (1968) *Punishment and Responsibility*, Oxford University Press.
Mabbott, J.D. (1939) 'Punishment', *Mind*, XLVIII, and in Acton, H.D. (1969) *The Philosophy of Punishment*, Macmillan.

APPENDIX

WHAT UTILITARIANISM IS

John Stuart Mill

A passing remark is all that needs be given to the ignorant blunder of supposing that those who stand up for utility as the test of right and wrong, use the term in that restricted and merely colloquial sense in which utility is opposed to pleasure. An apology is due to the philosophical opponents of utilitarianism, for even the momentary appearance of confounding them with any one capable of so absurd a misconception which is the more extraordinary, inasmuch as the contrary accusation, of referring everything to pleasure, and that too in its grossest form, is another of the common charges against utilitarianism: and, as has been pointedly remarked by an able writer, the same sort of persons, and often the very same persons, denounce the theory 'as impracticably dry when the word utility precedes the word pleasure, and as too practicably voluptuous when the word pleasure precedes the word utility'. Those who know anything about the matter are aware that every writer, from Epicurus to Bentham, who maintained the theory of utility, meant by it, not something to be contradistinguished from pleasure, but pleasure itself, together with exemption from pain; and instead of opposing the useful to the agreeable or the ornamental, have always declared that the useful means these, among other things. Yet the common herd, including the herd of writers, not only in newspapers and periodicals, but in books of weight and pretension, are perpetually falling into this shallow mistake. Having caught up the word utilitarian, while knowing nothing whatever about it but its sound, they habitually express by it the rejection, or the neglect, of pleasure in some of its forms; of beauty, of ornament, or of amusement. Nor is the term thus ignorantly misapplied solely in disparagement, but occasionally in compliment; as though it implied superiority to frivolity and the mere pleasures of the moment. And this perverted use is the only one in which the word is popularly known, and the one from which the new generation are acquiring their sole notion of its meaning. Those who introduced the word, but who had for many years discontinued it as a distinctive appellation, may well feel themselves called upon to resume it, if by doing so they can hope to contribute anything towards rescuing it from this utter degradation.*

The creed which accepts as the foundation of morals, Utility, or the Greatest Happiness Principle, holds that actions are right in proportion as they tend to promote happiness, wrong as they tend to produce the reverse of hapiness. By happiness is intended pleasure, and the absence of pain; by unhappiness, pain, and the privation of pleasure. To give a clear view of the moral standard set up by the theory, much more requires to be said; in particular, what things it includes in the ideas of pain and pleasure; and to what extent this is left an open question. But these supplementary explanations do not affect the theory of life on which this theory of morality is grounded – namely, that pleasure, and freedom from pain, are the only things desirable as ends; and that all desirable things (which are as numerous in the utilitarian as in any other scheme) are desirable either for the

*The author of this essay has reason for believing himself to be the first person who brought the word utilitarian into use. He did not invent it, but adopted it from a passing expression in Mr. Galt's Annals of the Parish. After using it as a designation for several years, he and others abandoned it from a growing dislike to anything resembling a badge or watchword of sectarian distinction. But as a name for one single opinion, not a set of opinions – to denote the recognition of utility as a standard, not any particular way of applying it – the term supplies a want in the language, and offers, in many cases, a convenient mode of avoiding tiresome circumlocution.

pleasure inherent in themselves, or as means to the promotion of pleasure and the prevention of pain.

Now, such a theory of life excites in many minds, and among them in some of the most estimable in feeling and purpose, inveterate dislike. To suppose that life has (as they express it) no higher end than pleasure – no better and nobler object of desire and pursuit – they designate as utterly mean and grovelling; as a doctrine worthy only of swine, to whom the followers of Epicurus were, at a very early period, contemptuously likened; and modern holders of the doctrine are occasionally made the subject of equally polite comparisons by its German, French, and English assailants.

When thus attacked, the Epicureans have always answered, that it is not they, but their accusers, who represent human nature in a degrading light; since the accusation supposes human beings to be capable of no pleasures except those of which swine are capable. If this supposition were true, the charge could not be gainsaid, but would then be no longer an imputation; for if the sources of pleasure were precisely the same to human beings and to swine, the rule of life which is good enough for the one would be good enough for the other. The comparison of the Epicurean life to that of beasts is felt as degrading, precisely because a beast's pleasures do not satisfy a human being's conceptions of happiness. Human beings have faculties more elevated than the animal appetites, and when once made conscious of them, do not regard anything as happiness which does not include their gratification. I do not, indeed, consider the Epicureans to have been by any means faultless in drawing out their schemes of consequences from the utilitarian principle. To do this in any significant manner, many Stoic, as well as Christian elements require to be included. But there is no known Epicurean theory of life which does not assign to the pleasures of the intellect, of the feelings and imagination, and of the moral sentiments, a much higher value as pleasures than to those of mere sensation. It must be admitted, however, that utilitarian writers in general have placed the superiority of mental over bodily pleasures chiefly in the greater permanency, safety, uncostliness, etc., of the former – that is, in their circumstantial advantages rather than in their intrinsic nature. And on all these points utilitarians have fully proved their case; but they might have taken the other, and as it may be called, higher ground, with entire consistency. It is quite compatible with the principle of utility to recognise the fact, that some *kinds* of pleasure are more desirable and more valuable than others. It would be absurd that while, in estimating all other things, quality is considered as well as quantity, the estimation of pleasures should be supposed to depend on quantity alone.

If I am asked, what I mean by difference of quality in pleasures, or what makes one pleasure more valuable than another, merely as a pleasure, except its being greater in amount, there is but one possible answer. Of two pleasures, if there be one to which all or almost all who have experience of both give a decided preference, irrespective of any feeling of moral obligation to prefer it, that is the more desirable pleasure. If one of the two is, by those who are competently acquainted with both, placed so far above the other that they prefer it, even though knowing it to be attended with a greater amount of discontent, and would not resign it for any quantity of the other pleasure which their nature is capable of, we are justified in ascribing to the preferred enjoyment a superiority in quality, so far outweighing quantity as to render it, in comparison, of small account.

Now it is an unquestionable fact that those who are equally acquainted with, and equally capable of appreciating and enjoying, both, do give a most marked preference to the manner of existence which employs their higher faculties. Few human creatures would consent to be changed into any of the lower animals, for a promise of the fullest allowance of a beast's pleasures; no intelligent human being would consent to be a fool, no instructed person would be an ignoramus, no person of feeling and conscience would be selfish and base, even though they should be persuaded that the fool, the dunce, or the rascal is better satisfied with his lot than they are with theirs. They would not resign what they possess more than he for the most complete satisfaction of all the desires which they have in common with him. If they ever fancy they would, it is only in cases of unhappiness so extreme, that to escape from it they would exchange their lot for almost any other, however undesirable in their own eyes. A being of higher faculties requires more to make him happy, is capable probably of more acute suffering, and certainly accessible to it at more points, than one of an inferior type; but in spite of these liabilities, he can never really wish to sink into what he feels to be a lower grade of existence. We may give what explanation we please of this unwillingness; we may attribute it to pride, a name which is given indiscriminately to some of the most and to some of the least estimable feelings of which mankind are capable: we may refer it to the love of liberty and personal independence, an appeal to which was with the Stoics one of the most effective means for the inculcation of it; to the love of power, or to the love of excitement, both of which do really enter into and contribute to it: but its most appropriate appellation is a sense of dignity, which all human beings possess in one form or other, and in some, though by no means in exact, proportion to their higher faculties, and which is so essential a part of the happiness of those in whom it is strong, that nothing which conflicts with it could be, otherwise than momentarily, an object of desire to them. Whoever supposes that this preference takes place at a sacrifice of happiness—that the superior being, in anything like equal circumstances, is not happier than the inferior—confounds the two very different ideas, of happiness, and content. It is indisputable that the being whose capacities of enjoyment are low, has the greatest chance of having them fully satisfied; and a highly endowed being will always feel that any happiness which he can look for, as the world is constituted, is imperfect. But he can learn to bear its imperfections, if they are at all bearable; and they will not make him envy the being who is indeed unconscious of the imperfections, but only because he feels not at all the good which those imperfections qualify. It is better to be a human being dissatisfied than a pig satisfied; better to be Socrates dissatisfied than a fool satisfied. And if the fool, or the pig, are of a different opinion, it is because they only know their own side of the question. The other party to the comparison knows both sides.

It may be objected, that many who are capable of the higher pleasures, occasionally, under the influence of temptation, postpone them to the lower. But this is quite compatible with a full appreciation of the intrinsic superiority of the higher. Men often, from infirmity of character, make their election for the nearer good, though they know it to be the less valuable; and this no less when the choice is between two bodily pleasures, than when it is between bodily and mental. They pursue sensual indulgences to the injury of health, though perfectly aware that health is the greater good. It may be further objected, that many who begin with youthful enthusiasm for everything noble, as they advance in years sink into indolence and selfishness. But I do not believe that those who undergo this very common change, voluntarily choose the lower description of pleasures in preference to the higher. I believe that before they devote themselves exclusively to the one, they have already become incapable of the other. Capacity for the nobler feelings is in most natures a very tender plant, easily killed, not only by hostile influences, but by mere want of sustenance; and in the majority of young persons it speedily dies away if the occupations to which their position in life has devoted them, and the society into which it has thrown them, are not favourable to keeping that higher capacity in exercise. Men lose their high aspirations as they lose their intellectual tastes, because they have not time or opportunity for indulging them; and they addict themselves to inferior pleasures, not because they deliberately prefer them, but because they are either the only ones to which they have access, or the only ones which they are any longer capable of enjoying. It may be questioned whether any one who has remained equally susceptible to both classes of pleasures, ever knowingly and calmly preferred the lower; though many, in all ages, have broken down in an ineffectual attempt to combine both.

From this verdict of the only competent judges, I apprehend there can be no appeal. On a question which is the best worth having of two pleasures, or which of two modes of existence is the most grateful to the feelings, apart from its moral attributes and from its consequences, the judgment of those who are qualified by knowledge of both, or, if they differ, that of the majority among them, must be admitted as final. And there needs be the less hesitation to accept this judgment respecting the quality of pleasures, since there is no other tribunal to be referred to even on the question of quantity. What means are there of determining which is the acutest of two pains, or the intensest of two pleasurable sensations, except the general suffrage of those who are familiar with both? Neither pains nor pleasures are homogeneous, and pain is always heterogeneous with pleasure. What is there to decide whether a particular pleasure is worth purchasing at the cost of a particular pain, except the feelings and judgment of the experienced? When, therefore, those feelings and judgment declare the pleasures derived from the higher faculties to be preferable *in kind*, apart from the question of intensity, to those of which the animal nature, disjoined from the higher faculties, is susceptible, they are entitled on this subject to the same regard.